DIVORCE MEDICS

FINALLY… There are answers for those facing divorce, separation, or an ending relationship.

By: *Bobbie Huskey*

Copyright © 2025 by Bobbie Huskey

All rights reserved. No part of this publication may be copied or reproduced in any format, by any means, electronic or otherwise, without prior consent from the copyright owner and publisher of this book. No AI Training: Without any way limiting the author's exclusive rights under copyright, any use of this publication to "train" generative artificial intelligence (AI) technologies to generate text is expressly prohibited.

ISBN # 979-8-9911433-2-5

Dedication

I dedicate this book to those who are hurting, despondent, and feel as though they have found themselves between a scalpel and the gurney. Allow God to be your "Great Physician." Trust in His wisdom, rest in His peace, and let His love guide you through every step of your healing journey. May the pages within be encouraging and guide you as you embark on a life of overcoming and success.

> "Fear thou not; for I am with thee: be not dismayed; for I am thy God; I will strengthen thee; yea, I will help thee; yea, I will uphold thee with the right hand of my righteousness."
>
> Isaiah 41:10 KJV

DIVORCE MEDICS
Edition 1   June 2025

Preface

Introduction

Chapter 1 ---------------Stages of Divorce/How it Happens--------1

Chapter 2 ---------------Stage 1 Shock--------------------------------17

Chapter 3 ---------------Stage 2 Denial-------------------------------31

Chapter 4 ---------------Stage 3 Anger------------------------------ 41

Chapter 5 -------------- Divorce Etiquette----------------------------51

Chapter 6 ---------------Stage 4 Bargaining-------------------------63

Chapter 7 ---------------House Hunting/ Forgiveness---------------71

Chapter 8 ---------------A New City----------------------------------83

Chapter 9 ---------------Stage 5 Depression/ Sadness---------------93

Chapter 10 ------------Surviving the Holidays-------------------- 103

Chapter 11--------Recovery Stage/Making the Shift---------------115

Bonus Chapters:

Chapter 12----------------Having Significance/Divine Purpose----123

Chapter 13----------------Health and Nutrition-----------------------129

Chapter 14----------------Budgeting/ Finances-----------------------135

Ending Note---151

Answer Key ---153

References ---157

Preface:

WARNING: This book offers new insight into divorce or an ending relationship, exploring its complexities and challenges. It uses powerful personal testimonies to guide you through each stage of the process. Get ready to view divorce from a new angle while discovering its truths.

Most families in America today have been touched in some way by divorce. According to data collected in 2014 by McKinley Irvin Family Law, the number of divorces per year is staggering, totaling as many as 876,000 or 16,800 divorces each week. (mckinleyirvin, 2012) According to the Gufford Law, more than 948,000 divorces were estimated to have occurred in 2021 alone. Firm,(2024)

Divorce can happen to anyone at any age, including those who have been married many years, and even after the children have left home. Most people do not know where to go or what to do with their lives, as all their plans have abruptly changed. It is not uncommon to battle emotions such as guilt, shame, loneliness, confusion, and hurt. Divorce Medics understands where you are and is committed to helping you navigate the stages of divorce, as well as providing answers to the many questions that arise along the way. You will also find personal glimpses into the lives of individuals at different stages and how they felt and dealt with situations. The goal of Divorce Medics is to help individuals understand that they are not alone and that <u>there are both answers and a meaningful purpose in life. You can rise above and live victoriously.</u> This is a Christian-based book;

regardless of your beliefs, it will provide valuable insight into divorce and how to navigate each phase.

This book has given me a deeper respect for every author and how each publication has its own unique story in some way. I also realize that writing is a process that requires time and diligence, and for me, it is only as the Master navigates my mind and hands.

Introduction:

Divorce can be very devastating, turning your life upside down while causing both physical and emotional pain. It is where new adjustments must occur, and the future is uncertain. Although each divorce is unique, they all carry what appear to be bottomless injuries, which often makes one question whether they will even survive. How do I know? I've been there, and thus, I will discuss many things that most would rather not.

For me, living single was not a choice but something I had to face abruptly and without warning. I went from a highly comfortable lifestyle to one of a more frugal nature. I felt betrayed and deserted. My whole world changed, as did my surroundings, employment, and purpose. As some friends dispersed, the feelings of failure and loneliness were almost more than I could bear, leaving me thinking, "Was life worth it?"

You have probably heard the adage "time heals all wounds," but it was just a band-aid for me. I felt I needed a team of medics to mend, hence the title Divorce Medics. Looking back, I remember how much trouble I had in focusing, and after months, I still battled with the tears; furthermore, I could not eat, I lost weight, and my health began to show it. I knew I had to put a plan into place to survive, so I did, and I now share it with you.

The first part of my plan was my support group, which I should have attended sooner, and it provided the foundation for this book. My sisters and children were instrumental in helping me through the initial shock. As a matter of fact, I could insert much of my journal into this book because one of my sisters, through encouragement, told me to "write EVERYTHING down because one day, I would use it." She did not realize those prophetic words were for this book. My other sister would call almost daily with encouragement and prayer. My two sons also played a massive part in my support team. These <u>individuals, along with my support group, became my core team,</u> which <u>EVERYONE</u> needs. I realized <u>we do not walk</u> <u>through this life alone, as we need each other every day, especially during troublesome times.</u>

> "For if they fall, one will lift up his companion." Ecclesiastes 4:10 NKJV

Because of this, I can now share how to overcome anxieties and depression while navigating through the challenges of divorce or broken relationships and go on to live a victorious life.

As you read through the following pages, may you find answers to many questions you may have and guidance on financial adjustments, everyday struggles. and how to transition into a new life.

I also encourage you to consider joining a support group where you can discuss your situation with others who share similar experiences, which can be beneficial. You will also find that the group leaders have valuable knowledge and trustworthy advice to offer on what you are going through. However, this book includes some self-help pages and resources if a group setting is not for you or is not available near you. Let God be your "Medic." He cares about you and your future.

In God's Word, it states,

> "Cast all your care on Him for He cares about you." 1Peter 5:7 AMP

> "He heals the brokenhearted and binds up their wounds." Psalm 147:3 AMP

God sees and understands every situation. He saw me, He sees you, and yes, He has a plan for your life.

[The names in this book are fictional, but the situations are real]

DIVORCE MEDICS

1

Stages of Divorce/ How it Happens

"Be strong and courageous ... The LORD himself goes before you…"

Deuteronomy 31:7-8 NIV

You may be like me and tempted to skip the preface or introduction of a book and dive straight into the content– I get it. Divorce is painful and overwhelming, and you likely want answers right away. However, just in case you're anything like me, reading the first few pages will give a clearer understanding of the book's content. By the time you reach the end of this book, you likely will find that your perspective on the situation has shifted meaningfully.

> [*I could hear the sirens going off in the back of my mind ... "What? Should I dial 911 or call the family? We need help; possible mini-stroke, he's sick!" These were the first thoughts that came to mind.*]

Stages of Divorce: Many people compare recovering from divorce to grieving the loss of a loved one. I believe this is valid because the relationship, in a sense, has "died." Recovering from a divorce can be just as painful as losing someone close to you. However, understanding the stages of divorce can make the recovery process smoother.

This chapter will discuss how divorce occurs and the grieving process that often accompanies it. We'll also briefly outline each stage of divorce, which we'll explore in more detail throughout the book. Not everyone will progress through the stages in the exact order presented; however, shock is always the initial phase.

1. Shock- Divorce shock is not the result of trauma but the reaction to a traumatic event. It is also known as a psychological shock or acute stress disorder. It is characterized by a strong disbelief and unwillingness to accept the situation. A person may refuse to believe the divorce is happening, often making excuses for their spouse's behavior and dismissing the seriousness of the problem. Those in shock may have difficulty sleeping,

feel physically exhausted, and struggle with concentration. It's common for people in this stage to describe themselves as "walking around in a daze."

2. Denial - In this phase, the individual refuses to accept the inevitability of the divorce. They may focus all their energy on trying to reconcile the marriage and solve its problems, often avoiding discussions of the divorce with anyone other than their partner.

3. Anger - At this stage, the individual often blames their spouse for the marriage breakdown, feeling betrayed and filled

with remorse. They may think that their spouse is "throwing it all away." Anger can lead to negative talk about the spouse to others, including the children. While bitterness may set in, the person may still harbor deep-down love for their partner, which leads to the next stage.

4. Bargaining- The individual in this phase may feel desperate, thinking, "I just want my life back." They'll do whatever it takes to save the marriage by bargaining with their spouse. They may even ask God to restore their relationship, hoping for a miracle that may not come to pass. This can lead to feelings of resentment towards God. It is important to note that God does not force anyone to act against their will, even if He disapproves of the situation. We'll explore this concept in more detail later.

5. Depression- Depression typically sets in when the reality of the divorce becomes undeniable. This stage is marked by extreme loneliness, sadness, and feelings of inadequacy. Depression may deepen once the partners separate. A person may become tearful and want to stay in bed all day or develop unhealthy eating habits. At times, individuals will turn to alcohol or drugs as a means to numb the pain.

6. Acceptance and Recovery- True acceptance (not just acknowledgment) is the first step toward recovery. It's when a person gains a deeper understanding of their life and situation. You may have heard the adage, "The dark skies

above will finally start to clear." The goal of this book is to guide you to the last stage, recovery. Before diving deeper, let's first explore how divorce happens.

How Divorce Happens, A Closer Look:

During a divorce, many people ask, "How does this even happen?" The dissolution of a marriage can happen to anyone, even to Christians. Marriages are not perfect and come with many demands. These demands, however, can deepen the marriage bond when God remains at the center of the relationship. But things can go wrong if life becomes unbalanced when one or both partners fail to keep God at the heart of their marriage.

After we receive Christ, walking with Him is a daily choice that requires continual learning and developing our love relationship.

> "As you, therefore, have received Christ Jesus the Lord, so walk in Him, rooted and built up in Him and established in the faith, as you have been taught, abounding in it with thanksgiving."
> Colossians 2: 6-7 NKJV

> "I am crucified with Christ: nevertheless, I live; yet not I, but Christ liveth in me: and the life which I now live in the flesh I live by the faith of the Son of God, who loved me and gave himself for me." Galatians 2:20 KJV

A healthy marriage is between two God-conscious people who learn to love each other despite challenging times. However, <u>if their guard is let down</u>, their carnal nature may take over in response to challenges. For example, issues such as finances or major decisions can lead to tension and heated discussions within the relationship. Couples may begin blaming each other, or one partner may internally hide their feelings, negatively affecting the marriage. Communication is often a precursor to marital issues.

Common Marital Problems:

1. Finances:

> One of the most common marital issues is finances. When finances are tight, the family will quickly feel the impact, and everyone becomes stressed. This may be due to job loss, changes in income, or, commonly, overspending. In some cases, overspending can become so severe that one partner may attempt to conceal their spending sprees, but it's usually uncovered. When this happens, it takes <u>two forgiving and willing</u> individuals to work through the issues, whether caused by dishonesty or stressful financial circumstances.

2. Intimacy:

> Sometimes, the bond that couples once shared begins to fade. They may live more like friends or roommates than a married couple. They follow the same daily routines with very few

variances. As intimacy diminishes, the deep connection that they once had can start to vanish. However, deep down, people desire physical touch and emotional fulfillment; when these needs are not met, one or both partners may seek it elsewhere, often leading to infidelity. Intimacy issues can manifest in many forms, whether physical, emotional, or personal. No matter the form, God has the answers, but it requires both partners to seek them out, which doesn't always happen.

3. Unmet Expectations:

Unrealistic expectations can cause significant strain in a relationship. People want everything to be perfect, and when it is not as envisioned, this can lead to disappointment and hurt. When disappointment creeps in, accepting that our partner has fallen short of our expectations is difficult. This can breed bitterness in one or both partners, challenging forgiveness and hindering the ability to move forward in the relationship.

4. An abusive relationship:

Abuse can take many forms, including verbal, mental, and physical, to name a few. Our Heavenly Father never intended for us to live in an abusive environment. If you or someone you know is in an abusive relationship, many programs, counselors, and online resources can provide support to survivors of abuse.

5. Unmatched Friends:

Some friends are not as connected to one partner in a marriage as they are to the other, for various reasons, which often creates tension. At times, the friend may try to "rescue" their pal from what they perceive as a miserable marriage, which only adds to the conflict. Furthermore, their opinions, outlooks, or beliefs can clash, putting a greater strain on the relationship.

6. Love and Appreciation for each other:

Many couples struggle with expressing love and appreciation for one another. Men are often driven by a deep desire to feel appreciated, while women want to believe they are loved. When these needs aren't met, tensions can build over time. Unfortunately, this unresolved issue can lead many couples to seek divorce before they can work through the problem.

In addition to these common complaints, society widely accepts divorce, making it easy for individuals to consider it. Some states even allow online divorces, with the process beginning within minutes. Given such simplicity, it's clear how many people in troubled marriages rush to the divorce courts to "settle things."

When evaluating the dissolution of relationships, many assume that a Christian family will never face such challenges. Still, statistics reveal that this is far from the truth. Just because a person is a

Christian does not mean that they are immune to the temptation of divorce or that they will never face it. However, if two people walk in the God kind of faith, the chance of a divorce is much lower. If two people are dedicated to that faith and believe in the covenant (a consecrated commitment before God) of marriage, they will not find themselves in divorce court.

An article from The Gospel Coalition states, "People who seriously practice a traditional religious faith- whether Christian or other- have a divorce rate markedly lower than the general population. <u>The factors making the most difference are religious commitment and practice.</u> (Stanton, 2012) In other words, those who are seriously committed to the Lord, attend church regularly, read the scriptures, and exercise spiritual growth (meaning faith with action) have a higher success rate in marriage. Nonetheless, when an individual's guard is let down, the enemy can step in. A person can become so deceived that they do not consider the consequences of divorce.

The adversary wants us to be deceived; however:

> "... Greater is He that is in you, than he that is in the world."
> 1 John 4:3 KJV

God has given us His "POWER," but individuals must remain <u>fully engaged</u> in that power to overcome daily challenges. We must be connected to the "power source" to receive the transfer or hear God's direction. Think of it this way... God is like the central power plant. In a power plant, power is distributed to multiple areas; however, if a line fails, an area may experience power interruptions. So, even though the power is available to all, not everyone may be able to receive the transfer from the primary source, as it has been interrupted. One must remain connected to receive God's power, which requires discipline and determination.

God's Word states:

> "Let us consider one another in order to stir up love and good works, not forsaking the assembling of ourselves together, as is the manner of some, but exhorting one another, and so much the more as you see the Day approaching." Hebrews 10: 24-25 KJV

God knew what each person would need to overcome the obstacles the enemy might send, but it requires perseverance. Because God has given us free will, choosing to follow Christ is a daily decision that requires ongoing commitment.

> "But grow in grace, and in the knowledge of our Lord and Savior Jesus Christ..." 2 Peter 3:18 KJV

> "For everyone who lives on milk is (doctrinally inexperienced and) unskilled in the word of righteousness, since he is a spiritual infant. But solid food is for the (spiritually) mature, whose senses are trained by practice to distinguish between what is morally good and what is evil." Hebrews 5: 13-14 AMP

When people are connected to God, who is our spiritual power source, they are more attuned to the enemy's schemes. But when a person becomes spiritually weak, their carnal nature takes over. <u>In that state, a person is more impressionable to the</u> <u>enemy's deception</u>. The trick of the adversary is nothing new, as it was first put into play with Adam and Eve in the Garden of Eden. They were given everything they needed and placed in a beautiful garden with only <u>ONE</u> commandment, which was:

> "but of the tree of the knowledge of good and evil, thou shalt not eat of it …" Genesis 2:17. KJV

However, they let their guard down (carnality set in), allowing the adversary to take advantage and deceive them into disobeying God. <u>The enemy convinced them to believe they</u> <u>would be better off choosing a different path,</u> one that led away from what God had planned for them.

Again, Christians must make a daily choice to follow God's Word, and in His Word, God lays out the plan for the family unit:

> "… what therefore God hath joined together, let not man put asunder." Matthew 19:6 KJV

This was God's plan, and Jesus explained it clearly. However, when He made this statement, the Pharisees, renowned legal experts and known for adhering to the "traditions of the fathers," questioned Jesus about it. They wanted to know if what Jesus was saying was true and why Moses permitted a writing of divorce.

> "When a man hath taken a wife, and married her, and

> it come to pass that she find no favor in his eyes, because he hath found some uncleanness in her: then let him write her a bill of divorcement, ..." Deuteronomy 24:1 KJV

Why would Moses command a divorce decree? They were testing Jesus. Jesus responded:

> "... Moses because of the hardness of your hearts suffered you to put away your wives: but from the beginning it was not so." Matthew 19:8 KJV

Believers must remain spiritually sensitive to God's Word and Spirit because the devil preys on confusion, negativity, and spiritual weakness to create chaos. We must always guard and protect our hearts, for no one is exempt! When either spouse becomes weak or frustrated with various situations, instead of turning to God, they may try to solve problems independently, which can lead them astray. Without a connection to Christ, people can make poor decisions.

Many people today continue to fall into deception repeatedly, and little by little, they harden their consciences until they feel it is ok to ignore God's Word. This is why the spouse seeking divorce can often walk away without remorse while the other partner is left in shock with their dreams shattered.

> "... in later times some will turn away from the faith, paying attention instead to deceitful and seductive spirits and doctrines of demons, (misled) by the hypocrisy of liars whose

> consciences are seared as with a branding iron (leaving them incapable of ethical functioning)." 1Timothy 4:1 AMP

Note that this does not mean the individual who has been deceived cannot turn from their misguided ways and, with a <u>repentant heart,</u> walk in God's love again. God always loves us and is ready to forgive.

> "For thou, Lord, art good, and ready to forgive; and plenteous in mercy unto all them that call upon thee."
> Psalms 86: 5 KJV

However, a person must be willing to turn from their wrong. The marriage could be mended in doing so, but this does not always occur.

I want to note that the adversary will often deceive someone into believing the lie that the divorce was solely their fault. It takes two strong individuals focused on family and God to keep a marriage intact. When someone lets their guard down, that is when the enemy steps in. God can heal a broken relationship if both partners are willing.

The Antidote

As mentioned, if two Christians grow in Christ and live in God's love, His love becomes the antidote to overcoming the adversary's deceptions.

"Love endures with patience and serenity, love is kind and thoughtful, and is not jealous or envious; love does not brag and is not proud or arrogant. It is not rude; it is not self-seeking; it is not provoked; it does not rejoice at injustice but rejoices with the truth. Love bears all things"

1 Corinthians 13:4-8 AMP

<u>So, what is the reason for divorce?</u>

When a person becomes preoccupied with the "things of this world" and gets distracted, they lose sight of God's ways and their families. As a result, they are misled in relationships and become deceived, which is why the divorce rates continue to rise.

However, <u>God offers great peace even during troubling times and desires to work in areas where we cannot.</u> While it may <u>be difficult now, God is greater than any challenge</u>. The initial jolt is extremely hard to bear and is discussed in the following chapter. I encourage you to give God one year, trust Him, and allow Him to guide you.

Self-Help Section

1. Divorce happens when a person allows their _____ to be let down.
2. A Christian family will never face the challenge of Divorce. True or False? _____
3. The adversary wants you to fail; however, greater is He that ___ _____ _____ than he that is in the world. 1John 4:3
4. God gives every person a free _____ to do as they choose.
5. A believer should stay sensitive to God's Spirit and Word because the devil will prey on confusion, negativities, and spiritual _____.
6. If two Christians live in God's love, His love is the _____ to overcoming the adversary's deceptions.
7. It may be difficult now, but God is bigger than your _____.

Notes_____

_____

_____

Points to Remember:

1. Not everyone goes through the different stages of divorce at the same time

2. There are common situations noted in divorce with deception

3. There is an Antidote to divorce

Prayer:

Heavenly Father, You know the person reading this book and their current situation. They may feel all this is too much to bear, but I pray that You would bind their inner wounds and comfort them. I ask You to guide, direct, and provide them with the answers they need to help them move forward in their recovery. A-men

---

DIVORCE MEDICS

2

Stage One-Shock

Somebody Dial 911...

[Should I dial 911 or call the family? I couldn't even fathom the words, "We need to dissolve our marriage." I became desensitized to the things around me, repeating, "Do you even know what you are saying?"

A few days before, we sat and chatted with friends until the conversation soon shifted to tragedy. An older couple was going through a divorce; we all sat there with our mouths gaping in surprise and disbelief. It seemed senseless. Why would they divorce after so many years together? I gaze at my spouse, feeling immense gratitude for our relationship. As everyone says, we are "the perfect pair." Then he slowly reached across the table for my plate, and I faintly heard the words, he is like a conspirator as Judas Iscariot. How strange, I wondered.

Later, as we drove home, we continued discussing the divorcing couple. "Why would they divorce now?" I asked. He just mainly sat in silence, but I would soon learn why. He had probably been thinking about this for some time, though I had no clue, and yes, even as he had reached across the table for my plate, a secret move, a conspirator's gesture.

His voice echoes as he explains, "I do not want it, but I feel this is best, so, yes, I want a divorce." I couldn't believe it.

Tearfully, I asked, "Do you even know what you're saying?" He sits quietly, looking down, as if hoping I would go away, refusing counseling or reconsideration.

This is how a seemingly perfect relationship ended in divorce. Nothing could have prepared me for the days that followed as my partner decided he wanted to dissolve our marriage.

After spending thousands on a wedding and years building friendships, everything changed in a matter of a few words. I must have gone 48 hours without sleep, tossing and turning, hoping it was all a dream. Then I'd wake up with a jerk, only to realize it was reality. During the day, I walked around in a daze, spending endless hours tearfully trying to reason with my spouse, hoping he would change his mind, only to hear the same response, "We just don't have enough in common."

Really? We had discussed all our differences before marriage. I was always faithful, a good housekeeper, and a supportive wife. Although I enjoyed my work, I quit my job to pursue my degree, for us, and this is where we landed. These thoughts swirled in my head repeatedly, but deep down, I felt the real separator was that I had deepened my relationship with Christ, and I would not give that up.]

"...take up their cross daily and follow me." Luke 9:23 NIV

[*In the following days, I frequently questioned myself: how can he walk away? What about all the years we shared and the memories we made? I thought about our family and friends. How could someone be so thoughtless of others? Trying to understand why my spouse wanted to end our relationship left me feeling as many others do–confused, disbelieving, and overwhelmed with turmoil and sadness.*]

Mary's Story:

Mary was a dedicated wife and mother of two. She and her spouse were actively involved in their church ministry. One afternoon, he came home and told her he had accepted a job requiring some travel but still allowing him time to serve in the church. Over the next few months, he began spending increasingly more time away from home and his family. One morning, while praying about her husband's job and increasing absence from home, their family portrait suddenly crashed to the floor. Mary knew immediately that God was preparing her for what was to come. Soon after, her husband called to say he had been thinking about their lives and felt unprepared for all the responsibility. He then admitted to being unfaithful and concluded that he wanted a divorce. Mary was shocked and could not fathom it; they had two beautiful children and were so blessed. Why would anyone want a divorce? She had no idea that he was unhappy. Even years after her divorce, she still doesn't understand what happened or what went through her husband's mind. He walked away, leaving her and the children to sort through the confusion and pain that never made sense.

John's Story:

John had been married for many years when his wife was unfaithful and filed for divorce. She then moved miles away, taking their child with her, making it difficult for him to visit. Over time, he established a healthy relationship with their child, but his life was forever changed. He knew he would never be able to regain the lost time, and deep down, he carried a great deal of anger.

Does any of this sound familiar?

If you look around at your neighbors, city, and, yes, even your church, you will likely notice that many families have been touched by divorce. Each of these marriages began with great promise, yet ended abruptly.

For me, as for many others, the reasons for divorce seemed frivolous. Yet people often look back and say, "I should have seen it coming." Divorce can take you by surprise.

The initial jolt that follows can be overwhelming, leaving you lost in confusion and grief. But from there, it becomes easier one step at a time.

Dealing with the Impact:

The initial jolt of a divorce is the hardest to face. Many symptoms, such as fatigue, mood swings, feelings of fear, sadness, loneliness, regret, hurt, irritability, forgetfulness, cognitive dysfunction, and prolonged sleep deprivation, accompany it. So, how does a person cope with the ramifications of the first phase of divorce while maintaining their sanity?

#1 Dealing with All the Emotions:

There is an overwhelming surge of emotions that can leave you feeling entirely out of control, pulling you down into what appears to be a dark, detached hole.

During a divorce, the myriad of emotions might feel like a wild ride down Dragon Tail Road in Tennessee–with no breaks! One moment, you might feel like you're starting to get it together, thinking you are headed toward a smoother road, only to hit the following curve: alternating between hope and helplessness. As far as you are concerned, you want the road and ride to end! You want control of your life again!!!

Press The Breaks!!!

To manage the emotional changes, many people begin the process of denial, which we will explore later. I know it's not easy, but things will slow down. <u>It's all about finding balance and identifying what benefits or encourages you during this time.</u>

Think Positive

Try to focus on positive things by reading uplifting books, watching feel-good movies, taking walks, or sitting in the sunshine. Doing so releases the chemicals serotonin and dopamine in the brain, which can brighten your day.

Staying Busy versus Taking Time Off

Some people may throw themselves into work as a distraction from the turmoil around them. While staying busy can be beneficial, taking some time off is a common need. Most facilities are very understanding and will work with employees who are going through a divorce. For example, when I realized my spouse was serious about divorcing, I couldn't bear living in the same house. It was just too painful, as I was constantly reminded of our life together and our families. I couldn't hold it together by being in the same environment. I needed time off to make a plan for moving. If you are in a similar situation, consider taking some time off. A day or two might make a big difference in your sanity.

A note of caution: Never pack up and leave home without first speaking with your lawyer. In some states, this could be abandoning the home, which may work against you. (except in abusive situations, leave for safety and speak with a lawyer). However, some people can make living arrangements with their spouse for a while, whether to save money or navigate a life transition, such as finishing college. There's no right or wrong answer; it's up to you to decide what works best. But know that you do have options. Once decisions are made, it can help to ease the pressure and create a more stable, independent feeling, which can boost your morale.

#2 Fear

Fear can often overshadow all other emotions during the initial phase of shock during a divorce. The fear of the unknown, starting over, and what your life will look like moving forward. You may also fear for your children (which we'll discuss later in the divorce etiquette section) and be concerned about finances (discussed in the finance section). Fear is a powerful force, but…

> "God has not given us a spirit of fear, but of power and of love and of a sound mind." 2 Timothy 1:7 KJV

Stand firm in your faith and write a plan. Much more will be covered later in this book, but for now, focus on getting enough rest and staying grounded.

#3 Getting the Rest You Need:

Managing your emotions and work simultaneously can become overwhelming if you have a full-time job and other responsibilities. As mentioned earlier, many people feel as though they're "walking in a daze" due to a lack of <u>sleep</u>.

Insufficient sleep worsens mood swings, fatigue, and poor judgment. Going 24 to 48 hours without sleep can make everything feel hazy and make it difficult to process what's happening around you. I distinctly remember functioning on 23 hours of sleep, hoping it was all a bad dream that I would soon wake up from.

Although I was a nurse, I was so distraught that I couldn't even figure out what medication to take or what to do to help myself rest at night. I was running on 2-3 hours of sleep; hence, I realized I had to make a change or I was heading toward self-destruction.

So, what do I do ... count sheep??

   ...Yep, did not work ...

The number one thing is prayer! It's the best treatment for sleep. Pray and surrender all your cares to God and cast the enemy out. Then ask for the angels of Heaven to surround you, and request restful sleep so you can wake up refreshed. Trust me... I tried everything. Sleep is a gift from God, and His desire is for us to rest well.

> "I will both lie down in peace, and sleep; for You alone, O Lord, make me dwell in safety." Psalms 4:8 NKJV

> "…. He gives His beloved sleep…" Psalms 127:2 NKJV

However, there are times when sleep feels almost impossible because, due to our humanity, we are so focused on other things. <u>If you're struggling, several natural products may help promote relaxation.</u> You may want to try relaxing teas, such as chamomile, which can help relieve anxiety, promote sleep, and ease muscle spasms and stomach discomfort. Other helpful teas include passionflower, ginger tea, or peppermint tea. Various types of teas are available to help with relaxation and promote sleep.

Another option is melatonin, a natural sleep aid that can help you fall asleep faster. (Melatonin is a natural hormone within the body that tells your brain to sleep.) Take as directed and always consult your healthcare provider before starting any new supplement, as I am not a doctor and cannot provide medical advice. If sleep continues to be a problem, consult your primary care physician.

#4 Cognitive Dysfunction:

PTSD

Post Traumatic Stress Disorder (PTSD) was first diagnosed in the 1970s in soldiers traumatized by war. Later, it was recognized in individuals affected by various types of abuse, accidents, life-threatening events, and, yes, even divorce. PTSD-like symptoms can develop during a divorce due to the activation of the body's "fight-or-flight" mechanism. This instinctive response tells our body to either stay and fight or flee from danger. You may have felt this in childhood if you were bullied or faced threats.

The fight-or-flight response is controlled by two systems in your body: the sympathetic and parasympathetic nervous systems. These systems control the fight-or-flight action. The sympathetic system kicks in during a stressful situation, while the parasympathetic system acts like a brake, returning the body to a calm, normal state. However, this brake is faulty for some individuals, leaving the body "stuck" in a heightened state of stress. Prolonged stress, or severe trauma, can lead to PTSD symptoms – what some refer to as "PTSD Post-Divorce."

Mark Banschick (2013) writes, "In the heat of a malignant divorce, you can develop PTSD. You may have flashbacks of abuse, or anticipate being attacked, many months down the road." Symptoms of PTSD may include <u>prolonged</u> anxiety, difficulty sleeping, nightmares, flashbacks, a constant state of being in a daze not related to sleep, lack of concentration, hopelessness, and avoidance of people, places, or any reminders of the past. If these symptoms persist, you should consult your physician.

Amnesia

Most people are familiar with amnesia, a condition in which an individual is unable to recall information, typically due to a brain injury or disease. However, there are different types of amnesia, and the type most commonly associated with divorce is localized amnesia– a condition where a person forgets specific events. In this case, the memories remain, but the person cannot recall them. Localized amnesia is more often diagnosed in women and is thought to function as a defense mechanism to block out painful or harmful memories. Sometimes these memories may resurface later; other times, they remain inaccessible. Localized amnesia can lead to feelings of detachment, depression, anxiety, mood swings, and relationship difficulties. If you suspect you may be experiencing localized amnesia, you should speak with your healthcare provider for guidance.

#5 Loneliness and Sadness:

Loneliness and Sadness are intertwined with feelings of isolation and hurt and can be carried over into later stages of divorce. While some may not experience these feelings immediately, they may arise as the divorce progresses, mainly discussed in chapter nine, the <u>Depression/ Sadness stage</u>.

For now, during the first stage of divorce, one of the most important things you can do is to find someone to confide in about the situation. It's crucial to choose a person who will listen non-judgmentally and calmly. Sharing your feelings with someone will help relieve the tension and pressure you may be carrying. As a word of caution, this is a space for you to process your emotions, not for venting about your ex.

It can also be beneficial to seek out a divorce support group. If you cannot find a group due to location or other factors, many online resources can provide valuable support. I <u>strongly encourage a support group</u>, because it offers a chance to hear from others who are going through similar experiences. In these groups, people share their coping strategies, offer support, and build meaningful connections. It's an opportunity to make new friends, have your voice heard, and offer your insights.

Additionally, helping others can shift the focus away from your struggles and reduce feelings of loneliness. Giving back to others boosts your well-being and enables you to feel less isolated. Support groups are therapeutic and educational, making them a valuable tool for navigating the transition through divorce.

Self-Help Section

1. During the "Shock" phase of divorce, "walking in a daze" is generally related to not getting enough _____.
2. List five things to manage during the shock phase: _____,_____,_____,_____,_____
3. It is essential to find someone to confide in about your divorce who will not be _____.
4. A _____ _____ can assist with the transitions in divorce.
5. A person could develop PTSD or Amnesia in divorce. True or False? _____.

Points to Remember:

1. Think positively
2. Stay busy
3. Get the rest you need
4. Find someone to confide in/ join a support group
5. Know that God is with you

NOTES:
_____

Points to Remember:

1. Stage 1 in divorce is shock/ usually the shortest stage

2. Divorce can evoke a range of emotions; focus on the positive.

Prayer

Heavenly Father, I ask that You protect me from the adversary, for he desires to rob me of Your joy. Hide me and those impacted by divorce under Your shadow, giving guidance, comfort, and strength each day. Help me to say the right words, choose the right choices, and make decisions that would allow me to follow Your direction and permit my life to flourish according to Your will. Amen

"Keep me as the apple of your eye; Hide me under the shadow of your wings ..." Psalms 17:8 NKJV

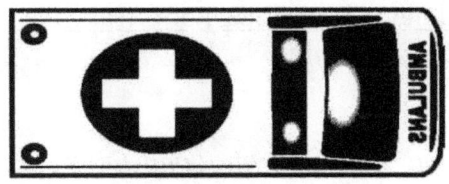

DIVORCE MEDICS

3

Stage Two Denial

[*The sun is slowly setting, and I must have been on the deck for hours. It's early July, and several days have passed. I'm sure my spouse will change his mind– he just spoke out of anger. I know my husband, and he would never do such a thing. If I wait, he'll completely retract his statement about divorce. After all, before we got married, we discussed how we never wanted the word "divorce" to be a part of our home. While praying and skimming through social media, I realized that most of my friends and family don't know my situation. I feel empty and lost. How could my life have gone so wrong? Maybe he'll change his mind. I thought I had done everything right to build a healthy marriage, yet here I sit with a shattered life. Where did it all go wrong? God, where are you?*]

Isn't this what most of us think when faced with strenuous situations? In times like these, it's easy to wonder where God is. Is He even aware of the problem? Does He care? Be assured, YES, He sees all, knows all, and is working on behalf of His children.

> "... I will never leave thee, nor forsake thee." Heb 13:5 KJV

[As the clock's hands tick by slowly, I only think. I continue to reflect on all that we shared. I blame myself for what I might have done to cause my partner to want to end our relationship, and I question all the "what ifs." You know the ones: "What if I had done this differently" or "What if I had approached things another way?"]

Most people wrestle with these "what if" questions. While it is a way to process everything, it reflects an underlying denial. At this point, individuals often criticize themselves for failed relationships or tragedies, which can lead to feelings of embarrassment or shame. At times, these feelings become overwhelming, and some will try to "numb" the pain by turning to drugs or alcohol. There's also a temptation to withdraw from family and friends and remain in a heightened state of anxiety for months. While it's understandable that you need time to adjust, <u>if these feelings persist</u>, consider contacting your medical professional, pastor, or counselor for guidance.

Having a failed relationship is not the fault of just one person, and you should not blame yourself for the divorce. It does not mean you are not "good enough," but the <u>DECEIVER</u> has interfered. A divorce does not reflect who you are or how God sees you. God calls His children precious, His jewels, and wonderfully made!

> "Because you are precious in My sight, you are honored and I love you, ..." Isaiah 43: 4 AMP

> "And they shall be mine, saith the Lord of hosts, in that day when I make up my jewels; …" Malahi 3:17 KJV

> "… for I am fearfully and wonderfully made; …"
> Psalms 139:14 NKJV

God's people are special!!! Don't let anyone tell you otherwise!

No one is to blame for the wrong decisions of others, and though <u>God may prick their heart, it does not mean that they'll listen</u>.
So, continue to move forward and refuse to live a life of regret. Do not let the enemy bombard your mind with negativity. I wish I had known earlier <u>how to send the enemy running by putting him back in his place.</u>

LESSON 1:

Verbally tell the enemy to leave and back it up with scripture. In Matthew 4, when the devil tempted Jesus, each time, Jesus responded with …

"It is written"… Matthew 4:4, 7, and 10, Jesus said... "Away with you, Satan! For it is written ..." Matthew 4:10 NKJV. Each time, He first declared, "It is written." So, verbally take authority and remind the enemy: 'It is written!'

> "I am fearfully and wonderfully made" Psalms 139:14 KJV

> … "you are precious in my sight" (Yes, you are!)
> Isaiah 43:4 AMPC
>
> "… For they shall be like the jewels of a crown,…"
> Zechariah 9:16 NKJV

I am considered God's Jewel… I am precious … It is written:

> "…I will never leave thee nor forsake thee." …
> Hebrews 13:5 KJV

The Lord has already won this battle because <u>it is written…</u>

> "…We are more than conquerors through Him…"
> Romans 8:37 NIV

Please keep this at the forefront of your mind daily, and when the enemy comes … send him packing! Exercise your spiritual senses! While studying at Ascension Life, Linda Miller taught a crucial four-step process to exercise our faith:

1. See the problem that you are faced with
2. Speak God's promise about the problem
3. See the victory… (visualize this in your mind)
4. Rejoice! (Miller, 2022)

We can walk in God's love and peace, no longer enslaved to fear and anxiety, no matter what we're going through or what the enemy tries to throw our way.

"And the peace of God, which passeth all understanding, shall keep your hearts and minds through Christ Jesus." Philippians 4:7 KJV

Refusal to Believe It is Happening:

Often, a person will deny that their divorce even exists and avoid discussing it altogether, or they may spend endless hours trying to salvage the marriage. This reaction is understandable, as most people resist change. Given that many changes are coming, it's easier to ignore the situation or hope it will just disappear. Denial is essential to the process because it allows a person to cope with their current reality. It serves as a defense mechanism, preventing them from feeling overwhelmed by what might otherwise be unbearable. It's normal and necessary for someone to slow down and take time to think. However, just because we deny what is happening doesn't mean it's not real.

In divorce, a person can choose how involved they want to be. For example:

1. Choose to deny it all, allowing your partner to take control.
2. Choose to control only a small percentage, with your partner controlling most of the divorce, or you can...
3. Choose to be fully engaged, sharing an equal 50/50 responsibility.

Since essential decisions must be made during this time, it will be necessary to come to terms with your divorce and address its challenges.

Challenges During Divorce:

Divorce presents various challenges, including dividing property, arranging parental time, determining child support if children are involved, managing finances, addressing tax issues, handling retirement benefits, and coordinating healthcare, among others. With so many obstacles, it's easy to see how a person could make costly mistakes by waiting and leaving things to chance. Even if the divorce isn't finalized immediately, it's better to be prepared and take control of the situation. The first thing to consider is seeking legal counsel. It doesn't obligate you to anything but can offer valuable insight. Some lawyers will take clients without requiring any upfront payment if finances are a concern.

[*It's been weeks now, and despite much discussion, my spouse has not changed his mind about proceeding with the divorce. Although I dread the thought, I realize our relationship may come to an end. Questions surface: "What will I do?" "Where will I go?" "What does my future look like?"*]

Coming to Terms with an Ending Relationship:

Accepting the end of a relationship is never easy, but there are steps that a person can take to navigate this complex process:

1. Talk about what went wrong. It can be helpful for individuals to sit down and talk with their ex, trying to understand each other's feelings and what went wrong in the relationship. This conversation allows both partners to be honest about their thoughts and plans. It doesn't necessarily mean that you will resolve everything, but having an open discussion during the early stages of divorce can help both parties. However, after the initial stages, continued talks, especially when one party is already determined to divorce, can delay the healing process. If you continue to invest energy and time into the relationship, you're not letting go and accepting the divorce, which can leave you in a repetitive cycle. The sooner you accept the end of the relationship, the sooner you can begin the healing process.

2. Write down all the pros, cons, and red flags of your ex and the marriage. When in a relationship, people tend to focus on their partner's positive qualities, often ignoring the red flags. During divorce, it's common for people to continue idealizing their ex, but journaling the "good, bad, and ugly" can help them see the relationship more clearly. Listing the positives and negatives enables you to realize that there were likely warning signs and that neither the person nor the relationship was perfect. This practice can be very eye-opening.

3. Consider ways to add value and enjoyment to your life. Reflect on the aspects of the relationship that brought you joy, meaning, and a sense of importance. For example, maybe you enjoyed

deep conversations with your partner. Finding someone to have similar discussions with can help fill that void. Or perhaps you enjoyed shared hobbies–consider joining a group or taking a class to connect with others who share your interests. It might also be as simple as taking long walks. Replacing those lost connections can be tricky initially, but taking proactive steps to restore those parts of your life can help you heal.

Godly Guidance:

Pray for God's guidance, asking to be led to those who can offer support during the divorce process. Consider those who have had similar experiences. Those who have already "been there" are often better able to help you come to terms with the relationship and guide you in the right direction. Your pastor, counselor, or support group can be a great resource. Most importantly, lean on God for peace, understanding, and comfort during this challenging time.

> "Peace I leave with you; my peace I give you. I do not give to you as the world gives. Do not let your hearts
> be troubled and do not be afraid." John 14:27 NIV

Self-Help Section

1. Many times, a person will deny that their divorce exists, which is part of the _____ stage.
2. Denial is a form of _____ mechanism.
3. Just because a person denies their divorce, it does not mean that it is not _____.
4. Some challenges during the divorce:
   _____, _____, _____, _____, _____, _____, _____
5. It may be beneficial to talk with _____ _____ during the early stages of divorce.
6. To help come to terms with everything, a person can write down the ____ ____ ____ as well as the "red flags" during the marriage.
7. A Christian support _____ or _____ is a good place to start for guidance.

Notes:_

_____

_____

Points to Remember:

1. Refuse to live a life of regret.
2. Send the accuser packing with the Word of God.
3. Do the things that add value and enjoyment to your life?
4. Come to terms with the relationship.

Lord, truly You are the "Good Shepherd." For those in this season of uncertainty, wrap them in Your arms of mercy and steady their hearts. Please give them the grace to take the time needed to process the changes and come to terms with their situation. Please provide them with the courage to face what is ahead and peaceful reassurance for a new beginning.

"The Lord is my Shepherd; I shall not want.
He maketh me to lie down in green pastures: He leadeth me beside the still waters. He restoreth my soul:..." Psalm 23: 1-3 KJV

DIVORCE MEDICS

4

Stage 3 Anger:

[As I gaze out the window, I ponder everything about to change. I can feel my anger grow, wondering how anyone could behave so selfishly toward their family. This has come as a whirlwind in my life, and now I must make choices I never thought I would face. I would like to know which direction to take and where it will lead me. I didn't ask for my life to be turned upside down, and it's hard to grasp. Everything plays over and over in my mind, retelling the story like a broken record where the needle is stuck, and I can't get it to move. The more it repeats, the stronger my anger becomes.]

While it is easy to feel like an innocent victim with gaping wounds, allowing anger, bitterness, and contention to take over is NOT the answer.

Wayne's Story:
Wayne recalls a conversation with his ex about their relationship. Even though he was a Christian, he became so outraged at one point that he yelled–something entirely out of character for him. Looking back, he knows that God forgives him, but he regrets letting his

anger get the best of him. He also finds it difficult to forget how easily he lost control.

It is easy to lose control when someone feels their world has been changed, and circumstances seem to rob them of their dreams and future. Still, when we allow a situation to spiral out of control, we give the enemy the upper hand. Anger is never the solution, and it can leave lasting scars. It's always best to walk away peacefully. One of the most important aspects during this time is to practice divorce etiquette, which is discussed in another chapter. Controlling your rage isn't just for everyone else, but for your well-being, too.

> "He who is slow to anger is better than the mighty…"
> Proverbs 16: 32 KJV
> "Good sense and discretion make a man slow to anger, and it is his honor and glory to overlook a transgression or an offense (without seeking revenge and harboring resentment) Proverbs 19:11 AMP

A person can feel angry, but in a way that doesn't control them or lead them to do something that they may regret.

How to Manage Anger

So, what should a person do when they become angry? How can they control their fury? There are many ways to cope with anger; here are a few suggestions:

1. The number ONE outlet is PRAYER!

2. Going to the gym.
3. Going for a long walk.
4. Hiking
5. Biking
6. Yoga
7. Engaging in creative activities such as painting, drawing, or playing a musical instrument. But number one, always stop to think and <u>pray.</u>

"Casting down imaginations, and every high thing that exalteth itself against the knowledge of God, and bringing into captivity every thought to the obedience of Christ;" 2 Corinthians 10:5 KJV

Through prayer, a person can forgive and control their thoughts, including anger, and choose to be obedient to Christ; it's a choice.

Letting go of anger doesn't mean agreeing with what the other person has done. It simply means acknowledging the hurt and deciding to move past everything.

Choosing to let go is not always easy, but learning to empathize with the other person can help you move past the anger and toward healing. When we understand <u>empathy, especially in the context of</u> divorce, forgiving the person who has wronged us becomes easier. Note that empathy involves having the love of Christ and compassion within us. Understanding how others feel leads to compassion, allowing Christ's love to grow in our hearts.

For example, when we "put ourselves in someone else's shoes," we begin to understand their emotions. <u>So, how can we empathize with our ex when we feel they are at fault</u>? While it may be true that our "ex" is responsible, it's essential to understand <u>"why."</u> When a person understands the "why," this can segue into empathy.

The "Why" of Divorce

In Divorce, "the why" is the same "why" that answers many of the questions that are so vague under challenging situations. Questions like, "Why did my partner leave?" "Why were they unfaithful?" "Why would someone tear apart a family?" All these questions circle back to the "why," which has existed since the time of Adam and Eve.

In the Garden of Eden, Adam and Eve had everything: abundant food, beautiful gardens, and a perfect life. God gave them one commandment... just ONE... not to eat from the tree of the knowledge of good and evil.

Then along came the cunning adversary, who deceived Eve. He told her that she wouldn't die if she ate the fruit but that her eyes would be opened, and she would be like God, knowing good and evil. When Eve saw how pleasant the fruit looked and how it could make her wise, she took it and ate it. After all, it looked good, so it had to be good... right?... NO! Eve went against God, and the deception was complete. She then involved Adam, and they were both cast out of the garden. Their lives were changed forever because of this deception.

When reflecting on this situation, it becomes easier to have empathy for them. <u>They were deceived</u>. Similarly, if someone is deceived by the "grass is greener on the other side" syndrome and decides to leave their partner, we can have compassion for them, knowing that <u>their lives will be changed forever as a result</u> <u>of the deception</u>. So, the answer to the "why" of all the questions is <u>deception.</u>

By understanding this, we can more easily empathize with those who leave, knowing that they, too, have been deceived. The love of God works through compassion.

> "Be ye kind and compassionate to one another, forgiving each other, just as in Christ God forgave you." Ephesians 4:32 NIV

In divorce, we can show compassion by recognizing that the partner who left made a decision to end the marital union, but they have been influenced or misled by the adversary.

> "For we wrestle not against flesh and blood, but against principalities, against powers, against the rulers of the darkness of this world…" Ephesians 6:12 KJV

The Abusive Relationship:

It's important to note that there are times when a person must leave an abusive situation for their safety. This is a different circumstance where the abuser has caused the separation. In these cases, the innocent partner left not due to deception but because of abuse.

The Power of Empathy

One thought comes to mind about Jesus on the cross. As He looked down, He said:

> "Father forgive them for they know not what they do..." Luke 23:34 KJV

In a sense, I believe He was acknowledging that the abuser, too, had been deceived. Even though they had crucified Him, Jesus had compassion and prayed for them. <u>This is the kind of Godly love that the Father gives, and it can only be received through His Spirit, who works within us.</u>

Empathy is powerful! Empathy can help us release our anger, surrender the situation to God, and experience forgiveness. In doing so, we release ourselves from the chains of anger and allow healing to begin. But what happens when we act impulsively out of anger? We all have our moments... Be quick to say 'I'm sorry,' quick to believe, and quick to forgive ...As the saying goes, no one is perfect.

We all make mistakes, sometimes losing control of our anger. The key is learning to manage that anger so it doesn't control you. When a person has a fit of rage, it's often followed by self-condemnation; thoughts like, "You're a loser," "You always mess up," or "You can't control yourself." Condemnation judges and sentences a person, but God's Word says otherwise:

> "There is therefore now no condemnation to those who are in Christ Jesus, who walk not after the flesh, but after the Spirit." Romans 8:1 KJV

If you are a child of God, admit you messed up, trust in His Word, and believe that His promises are true. Then, forgive yourself and move forward. Christ has already forgiven you! This is the reason Christ went to the cross. Rev. David Huskey once said:

> "When we stray from the Spirit of God, we can quickly recognize our mistake and ask God for help. With a repentant heart, we can then step back into walking in the Spirit of God's love."

If someone becomes stuck in condemnation, they cannot move forward to a happy and healthy life. So, stay positive. Focus on positive thoughts, engage in uplifting activities, and surround yourself with positive people. Learn to laugh! Read comic books, watch comedies, or view funny videos. Positive thoughts release serotonin, a neurotransmitter associated with feelings of contentment and joy. By making these minor adjustments, you can become a happier person in Christ.

Self-Help Section

1. List some Positive Outlets for Anger:

    a. _____

    b. _____

    c. _____

2. What is the number one thing that a person can do to relieve the anger?

    _____

3. In Divorce, the "why" is the same "why" that answers a lot of questions. What is this "why?"

    _____

4. To have empathy is to have

    _____

5. If one engraves positivity into their mind, it releases a "feel good" hormone called _____

Notes:
_____
_____
_____

Points to Remember

1. Manage Anger so it does not have control over you
2. The "Why" of divorce/ understanding deception is key
3. There is power in empathy

Prayer

Lord, thank you for loving us with an everlasting love that never changes. Help us to love others as you would have us to and to show compassion while letting go of resentment, bitterness, and unforgiveness that we may walk as you would have us to every day. Amen

DIVORCE MEDICS

5

Divorce Etiquette

Let's face it: with all the feelings of hurt, disbelief, uncertainty, and the complex mix of emotions that come with it, divorce can make anyone "hot under the collar." Even individuals with the highest standards and morals can be nudged into the "get-even" mindset. Let me say, "You may think it, but don't act on it!" Just as there are rules in marriage, there are also rules in divorce, also known as "divorce etiquette." Yes, etiquette is vital for everyone's sake, including yours.

Mia's Story
Mia learned that her spouse wanted a divorce. After the initial shock, Mia began to adopt a "get even" mentality. She withdrew excessive funds from their checking account, feeling she deserved it; after all, this was all <u>his</u> fault. She then stopped allowing the children to see her "soon-to-be-ex" because he was the one who had broken up their family. However, who was Mia hurting? Let's think about this: By not allowing the children to see their dad, yes, she was hurting him,

but she was also hurting the children. A "get-even" mindset only leads to more harm than good. The bottom line is ... don't go there.

> "...be of one mind, live in peace; and the God of love and peace shall be with you. 2 Corinthians 13:11 BSB

Returning Valuable Gifts

Families will often give extravagant gifts. Their intention is for you both to enjoy these gifts together. However, the underlying truth is that the gift is typically meant for a blood relative. When a divorce occurs, assets are typically divided 50/50. If part of your "50" includes a gift from your ex's family, you may want to consider returning it. By keeping the gift as part of your "50," you are doing the relatives an injustice and creating further contention. God's Word states that the fruit of the righteous <u>is sown in peace</u> of them that make peace.

> "For where envying and strife is, there is confusion and every evil work: But the wisdom that is from above is first pure, then peaceable, gentle, and easy to be intreated, full of mercy and good fruits, without partiality, and without hypocrisy. And the fruit of the righteousness is sown in peace of them that make peace." James 3:16-18 KJV

> "If it be possible, as much as lieth in you, live peaceably with all men." Romans 12:18 KJV

To keep peace, it's best to return valuable gifts. You never want to prolong a dispute in divorce court over simple items that you may be required by law to return anyway.

Children and Divorce:

When children are involved, the priority is to reassure them that both parents love and will always be there for them. Let's face it, when you are going through divorce, it can be overwhelming, and with so focus on survival and what comes next, you often forget about the impact on the kids. No one is perfect, and we all make mistakes; however, be patient with yourself and try to maintain a stable and reassuring environment for them.

Mind Your Words:
Always be prayerful about what you say, not just what you do. Never speak negatively about your ex-spouse or lambaste each other in front of the children. This hurts them; remember, they love you both and may struggle with whom they should be loyal to. The answer is BOTH! They should not have to choose. The divorce is between you and your partner– do not use the children as part of the battleground. If your ex is not a good person, your children will recognize this as they grow older. Let them form their own opinions without persuasion. I know this is difficult, but it's not impossible. Negativity only fuels the fire and builds insecurities in the children, so be mindful of your words.

"The soothing tongue is a tree of life, but a perverse tongue crushes the spirit." Proverbs 15:4 NIV

Children and Insecurities:

Children of divorce could develop insecurities that go unaddressed because they're not always visible. Think about it: they're transitioning from a family unit to a single-parent home with one income. Not only is one parent absent, but the family budget is tighter, and though it's hard to admit it, they are affected. It is a good practice to reassure them consistently, even if they don't show signs of insecurity.

Statistics often show that children may experience anger, fear, anxiety, depression, low self-esteem, resentment, or have a drop in their school grades due to their emotions and insecurities. This can be subtle and easily overlooked, especially when the parent is preoccupied with the divorce. Consider speaking with your children often about their emotions and how they are doing. You may want to consider consulting a counselor; many schools also have counselors on staff.

Rearing Children in a Christian Home:

Children in divorce situations will have many questions. Pray and study to ensure you have the answers. Several websites and books are dedicated to helping parents and children navigate the divorce process.

Here are a few resources I'd like to share, though there are many others:

1. What Are the Effects of Divorce on Children https://www.familymeans.org/effects-of-divorce-onchildren.html (Means, 2024)
2. Children and divorce: Helping kids after a breakup https://mcpress.mayoclinic.org/parenting/tips-for-coparenting-after-divorce/ (Hannah Mulholland, 2024)
3. How Might Divorce Affect My Children http://yourdivorcequestions.org/how-might-divorceaffect-my-children/
4. The Truth About Children and Divorce: Dealing with the Emotions So You and Your Children Can Thrive by Robert E. Emery, Ph.D. / Jan 31, 2006
5. Mom's House, Dad's House: making two homes for your Child by Isolina Ricci, Ph.D. | Nov 18, 1997.

Social Media

Social media platforms, including Facebook, Instagram, TikTok, LinkedIn, Snapchat, and X, have billions of followers worldwide. These platforms allow users to share their videos, photos, and personal thoughts. However, these sites are increasingly becoming battlegrounds, and just because the Bill of Rights grants us freedom of speech, it doesn't mean you should take to social media to lambast your ex. Also, you risk being banned from social networks or making false statements, which could be considered defamation and result in civil liabilities.

Additionally, with billions of viewers, it's possible that your children, your boss, or your potential employer could see your post, creating new issues. Many companies now research potential hires on social media to assess whether they are a good fit for the organization. A company may see your post and deem you an inappropriate candidate, leading them to pass you over for the job.

Social media can be a great tool – use it to your advantage, not disadvantage, and stay true to your character. When you need to express your deepest feelings about your situation or divorce, consider journaling or speaking with a counselor instead. This will help you emerge stronger and healthier, ultimately coming out on top.

Social Outings/ Events

Most married couples develop friendships as a duo, and after divorce, attending social events can feel a little awkward. Nonetheless, when someone ventures out alone, they may be tempted to defend themselves regarding their ex. Feeling emotional and wanting to talk about your ex with friends is a perfectly understandable reaction. However, while it's helpful to vent, being mindful of your dual friends is essential. It's best to remain careful about what you say to mutual friends.

If you must discuss your feelings with someone, consider speaking to your pastor, a counselor, or someone who doesn't know your spouse– perhaps find a support group. These people are more likely to listen with an open mind. It is always best to refrain from using old friends as an outlet to vent, as doing so could damage your friendships.

Your friends may seem distant or even avoid you and your ex during the early stages of the annulment. Don't take it personally, as it is not about you. Your friends may not wish to be involved, and since they do not fully understand the situation clearly, they may choose to remain quiet. It's like the little girl showing her grandpa a hidden picture workbook, asking him to find the hidden dog. While she quickly found it, her grandpa, whose vision was dim, couldn't see it as easily and remained quiet. Similarly, your friends may decide to stay silent because they don't see the situation clearly, and as the saying goes, "There are always two sides to every story." Although they may be silent now, it's not a reflection on you. Continue praying and trusting God.

> "Do not be anxious or worried about anything, but in everything (every circumstance and situation) by prayer and petition with thanksgiving…" Philippians 4:6 AMP

Meeting with Your Ex

At some point, you may need to meet with your ex. While this may be unpleasant and stir up mixed emotions, don't let it catch you off guard. If you decide to proceed, consider creating a list of the points you want to address. If your ex scheduled the meeting, try to get the agenda in advance. Once you know the points they wish to discuss, use this as a guide for your conversation. Most importantly, stick to the agenda points. This will help you stay on track and manage any unpleasant emotions that may arise.

It's ok to say no or to postpone the meeting if you're stressed, worried, sleep-deprived, or anxious. It's better to reschedule than to attend a meeting when you're not in the right state of mind, which could lead to being rude, frustrated, or emotional, only to regret it later. Schedule meetings when you feel more confident and prepared. Remember, your goal is to address the matters at hand, not to rehash the past or "set them straight"; it is to cover the points established and resolve the issues you would like to discuss.

Creating Boundaries

After a divorce, it can be challenging to define clear guidelines for each of you to follow. After all, you were married and likely are not accustomed to having ground rules with your spouse. Once divorced, it's time to detach and recognize that you are now two individuals living at separate addresses. Here are a few suggestions for setting healthy boundaries:

- Call or text first: Don't appear unannounced at your ex's front door. This happens more often than you might think, but it's not polite to show up at someone's home unannounced, as if you still live there; remember, <u>it is</u> <u>no longer your address</u>.
- Time with the children: When spending time with the children, drop them off and remain in the vehicle. If your ex walks out to

your car, as mentioned earlier, keep conversations short and to the point. To avoid setting yourself up for further issues, stay calm and remove yourself from the situation as quickly as possible. Be mindful that the children may be nearby and listening.

- Children's events: Both parents should be able to attend events involving the children. Facilities are usually large enough that you don't need to sit near the other parent and vice versa. Please refrain from bringing your "new friend" to show off – it's poor etiquette. Remember, you're there to support your children, not to make a statement.

- Spending sprees: Spender beware…. Don't plan big shopping sprees with the children to make your spouse look bad or sway their opinion. This happens more often than you think, and as children grow, they begin to see through these tactics. They may even turn against the big spender trying to "buy their love," so remain fair.

It's in your best interest in the long run.

- Raising children: Strive to stay on the same page regarding parenting; you may have different beliefs, but keep Christ as the center. Avoid judging the other parent too quickly, as children often use their parents against each other to get their way. Never speak negatively about your ex to your children. If you disagree on an issue, schedule a time to call or meet with your ex to discuss it.

- Be independent: If you've spent many years focusing on your family and spouse, adjusting to life alone can be a frustrating experience. Try to be independent and avoid codependency on your ex-spouse. Co-dependency can manifest in simple ways, such as asking them to repair things for you, requesting financial assistance (beyond their responsibility), or seeking their opinion on matters that don't involve the children. Instead, reach out to a friend, a co-worker, or someone from a local church. Churches often offer support groups for those experiencing divorce. When you ask your ex for help, it doesn't allow you to fully separate from the relationship; instead, you feed their self-esteem while easing their conscience. If your ex constantly asks for help, learn to say no and set boundaries.
- You now have a new life, let go of the past and move forward.

Self-Help Section

1. Having a "get even" mindset will only give your ex _____

2. Be of one mind, live in _____, and the God of love and peace shall be with you. 2 Corinthians 13:11

3. Negative words will bring _____ in our children during divorce.

4. The soothing tongue is a tree of life, but a perverse tongue _____ the spirit. Proverbs 15:4

5. I now have a new life in front of me, and as far as the past, I am going to just "____ __ of __"

NOTES:
_____
_____

Points to Remember:

1. Etiquette: Put the "get even" spirit to the side

2. Children and divorce: watch for insecurities/ both parents can be involved

3. Manners and words make a difference for everyone involved

4. Create boundaries

Prayer

Heavenly Father, I recognize my anger and ask you to forgive me and help me to walk in love through your Spirit. Give me the wisdom I need to deal with every situation I face and the ability to love as you would. Thank you for your forgiveness, mercy, and kindness, which are renewed in me daily. A-men

> "For I know the Plans that I have for you, declares the Lord, plans to prosper you, and not harm you, plans to give you hope and a future." Jeremiah 29:11 NIV

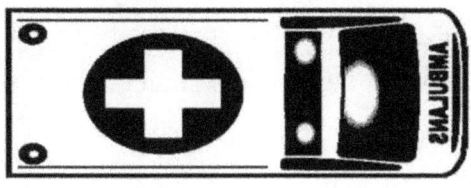

DIVORCE MEDICS

6

Stage 4 Bargaining

[*It has been weeks, and we sit on the sofa discussing the inevitable. We talk about counseling, but my spouse's response is always the same: counseling doesn't work. Then come the "whys" with his same repetitive answer: "Too many differences." It all feels so rhetorical. There's no rationalization to any of it, so I meander to bed, zigzagging along the way, before collapsing into bed. I feel both mentally and physically exhausted from trying to change things.*]

Bargaining during a divorce is typically not just about losing the marriage but also about maintaining family stability and keeping everything "normal." The bargainer does not understand the "Why" their partner decided to leave. They often focus on the idea that life would be perfect if it weren't for this one thing.... DIVORCE! They ponder how everything will change: there will be only one person in the home, finances will change, and daily tasks will now fall on one person. The burden becomes overwhelming, prompting the person to try bargaining repeatedly. Bargaining is a

<u>natural process</u> as the individual attempts to save the marriage, and rightfully so. These negotiation strategies have, at times, kept marriages together.

However, it <u>takes two willing partners for this to work</u>. No one can predict how long a person will remain in this unaltered stage; for some, it may take weeks, while for others, it may take months. In most cases, the partner who is leaving has already envisioned a different, perhaps better, life, which stems from the "deceiver mentality." Since they are convinced that this new course is right, they often resist reconsidering. As a result, the divorce progresses forward. Although the reluctant party sees their divorce advancing, the fear of letting go can prolong the bargaining phase.

There are various ways to bargain, which may involve changing certain habits or behaviors. For example, a person may have poor spending habits, so they relinquish all their credit cards to their spouse, or the person who has frequent outings with friends three nights a week might agree to cut it down to one night a week. The bargainer believes that altering their way of life will make their partner happy and persuade them to stay in the marriage. Other forms of bargaining may include changing religious beliefs, hoping that if they align with their partner's beliefs, the relationship will be saved. It could mean taking a new job. The list could go on, but the main point is that all these changes are made to get the partner to reconsider the relationship. Unfortunately, it does not always work, leading to the realization that the marriage may end. A deep sense of grief may follow this recognition.

Grief in the bargaining stage is when a person begins to question everything about the relationship, including their time together and what went wrong, then repeatedly replays it in their mind. This grief can also be a precursor to depression, which we'll discuss in the next chapter. The grieving individual begins asking all the "what ifs": "What if I had gone to the movies more?" "What if I had cooked more?" "What if I had kept the house cleaner?" "What if I had tried harder?" A person may convince themselves that the divorce was their fault, even though their partner wasn't willing to go to counseling. These premeditated thoughts lead to feelings of bereavement and grief. The person may feel unlovable or as if something is wrong with them. Since they have convinced themselves that the divorce is their fault, this can fuel the bargaining cycle, which becomes a vicious cycle.

Alex Admitted:
"I was still bargaining for approximately two years. This included negotiation strategies, along with multiple counseling sessions, before I realized that the relationship between us would not work out. It took God to help me accept it and move to freedom." Focus on the things of God; seek His wisdom and have faith in Him.

> "Thou wilt keep him in perfect peace, whose mind is stayed on thee: because he trusteth in thee." Isaiah 26:3

> "Trust in the Lord with all your heart and lean not on your own understanding." Proverbs 3:5 NKJV

The Word of God reveals that having a relationship with God and leaning on Him can bring about change. In the book of Job, he lost everything, and his friends were judgmental toward him. The Bible tells us that God became upset with Job's friends because they did not represent Him accurately to Job. In the end, Job prayed for his friends, and that's when things began to change for him.

> "… the Lord restored his fortunes and gave him twice as much as he had before." Job 42:10 NIV

> "… you have heard of Job's perseverance and have seen what the Lord finally brought about. The Lord is full of compassion and mercy." James 5:11 NIV

If a child of God remains persistent during challenging times, staying faithful and unafraid, they will witness how the Lord's compassion and mercy transform their situations.

There are many accounts in the Bible where situations seemed impossible or were discouraging, but were changed through faith. For instance:

- By faith, Moses led the children of Israel out of Egypt, Exodus 12:32.

- By faith, Gideon took a small army and won the battle against the Midianites, Judges 7.
- Sarah conceived, Genesis 21:2
- By faith, Esther saved a Nation, Esther 8:7-8
- By faith, Peter healed a lame man through the power of God, Acts 3:1-7
- By faith, the sinner is saved, Mark 16:16

These are just a few examples. Be encouraged; though things may look bleak, God has a beautiful plan.

Sometimes, we must learn to trust in God, even when we can't see how the situation will work out for the best. Remember Joseph in Genesis 37-44: he was sold into slavery by his brothers and then thrown into a dingy, dirty prison. He likely felt unloved, rejected, and discouraged. Yet, as his story unfolds, God was putting things into place behind the scenes. In the end, Joseph became second only to the king, and through him, Egypt, his family, and the Israelites were saved. Joseph trusted God, even when he was at his lowest. Joseph operated in faith, not fear. Faith opens the heart of God; fear operates through the adversary. It is easy to fall into fear when facing divorce with so many challenges, but resist the devil; through prayer, the Holy Spirit will guide you. Then, it is up to you to take action and follow Him. If you have not received Christ as your Savior and been "born again," please refer to the end of chapter 12. God wants to repair your life. We serve an awesome God working behind the scenes in our discouragements, disappointments, and challenges, making a way.

> "And we know that all things work together for good to them that love God, …" Romans 8:28 KJV

<u>Trust in the Lord and give your burdens to Him</u>. Realize that you are not responsible for the end of a relationship when you've tried everything to make it work.

If you stay stuck in the bargaining stage, clinging to the relationship, you will prevent yourself from moving forward and achieving a fresh start. Be determined and have faith–

There is a purpose for you, and YOU ARE LOVED!

> "Now may the God of hope fill you with all joy and peace in believing, that you may abound in hope by the power of the Holy Spirit." Romans 15:13 NKJV

There is a light ahead of me

Self-help section

1. It takes _____ willing partners for a marriage to work.
2. The bargaining is not only due to the loss of the marriage, but they are trying to keep everything as "_____" as possible.
3. Types of bargaining may include:

    a. _____
    _____

    b. _____
    _____

4. Bargaining could go on for years, where a person is "stuck" in this stage.   T or F
5. All things will work for the _____ of those who love God.
6. Be determined, have _____ ; you are loved.

Notes:
_____
_____

Points to Remember:

1. Bargaining is a natural process, but it takes two to make things work.

2. Prayer changes things/ Have faith

3. All things work for the good to them that love God/ there is purpose.

PRAYER:

"Search me, O God, and know my heart; Try me, and know my anxieties; And see if there is any wicked way in me, And lead me in the way everlasting." Psalms 139:23 NKJV

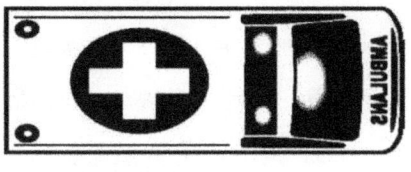

DIVORCE MEDICS

7

HOUSE HUNTING/ FORGIVENESS

"Draw near to God, and He will draw near to you..."
James 4:8 NKJV

God desires to guide us, but we must step out of our comfort zones and allow Him to take the lead. I learned this early in my divorce. Amidst the turmoil, I prayed for guidance on finding employment and a place to call home, and everything fell into place flawlessly.

[I prayerfully began searching for a place to live and a job. I scoured the internet daily, browsing rental listings and job postings, while reminding myself that God is my help in times of need. After hours of searching, I had no luck. I am relocating to a college town, and the rentals tend to go quickly! As I was ready to give up for the evening and turn the computer off, I felt nudged to look again. "Why should I try again, Lord?" I wondered. "Didn't I just search?" However, I wanted to ensure I wasn't missing God's direction, so I gave it one last try. As I searched the listings again, suddenly, a house appeared that had not been there before. It was slightly above

my price range, but I decided to investigate further. I quickly called my son, knowing he was familiar with the area. He urged me to go and look at the house right away. He felt it would rent quickly, and most likely within the next 24 hours. As I drove to the location, I repeated a scripture in my mind.]

"If God be for us who can be against us … if God be for us who can be against us…" Romans 8:31 KJV

The Perfect Place

[I needed a place to live, and I knew that God could help me find it, so I kept repeating the scriptures. My sister and son met me at the house; it was stuck in the 80s. There were a few repairs needed, which complicated things. I think, "I don't understand, God, you showed me this house, but there are too many repairs to be done." My son then informed us that he had seen another house on the way. Someone had just placed a "For Rent" sign in the front yard, not too far from the house we are viewing. We all rush to the second house to take a look and, hopefully, get a contact number. When we arrived, a man was working outside the property, so I inquired about it. The home was a 3-bedroom, 2-bath rental and had just become available. He also mentioned that the homeowner would arrive soon to inspect the house. Sure enough, the owner arrived within 15 minutes, and we conversed about the property. The home was

located within a few miles of my new job and shopping area, which was convenient for me. Although it wasn't perfect, I realized this home was a good fit for me. I was amazed to witness God's intervention on my behalf; not only did I get to view the house on the spot, but the owner also agreed to rent it to me for less than the listed price, and then he sweetened the deal by including the washer and dryer! Furthermore, he offered to take care of the yard work! In my heart, I knew that through God's miracle-working power, He had directed me to this place.]

The Perfect Job:

[As I searched for employment, I felt God leading me to a particular facility. Therefore, trusting in Him, I went to the business. When I arrived, I couldn't find anyone in the office; not a single person was there. I looked around: at the front desk, down the hall, glanced into a few other offices, then back up the hall towards the nurses' station ... but no one was there; nope, not a soul. After waiting and meandering around for a while, I was about to leave when a cheerful woman came down the hall towards me. I began to ask about the HR Department, or if I could speak to the Director of Nursing. She was very kind, and we conversed for some time; then, she asked if I would return in an hour for an interview. My first thought was, who is this person scheduling an interview for me? She appeared to be an office worker, not wearing a uniform, which puzzled me. Then, she introduced herself as the Director of Nursing! God had led her directly to me and no one else! God knows what you need, where to

send you, and who to put in your path at just the right time. I had a job within 2 hours of God first speaking to me. Let me add that I worked at that facility for some time, and the halls are NEVER empty, nor is the front office ever unattended. I had realized that God orchestrated this meeting for me, but I had to be willing to pray, trust, and be sensitive to His Spirit guiding me.]

> "Trust in the Lord with all thine heart; and lean not unto thine own understanding." "In all thy ways acknowledge Him, and He shall direct thy paths." Proverbs 3:5-6 KJV

> "I will instruct thee and teach thee in the way which thou shalt go: I will guide thee with mine eye." Psalm 32:8 KJV

It's all about having a relationship with God, fully trusting Him, and placing our lives in His hands, knowing He will direct us and lead us where we need to go.

[I had finally found a new job and a rental in a new city. As I thanked God, I still couldn't believe how quickly things were changing in my life, and yet, sadly, my marriage was coming to an end.]

Unforgiveness: (A Nasty Intruder)

Forgiving someone does not always come easily. You may ask yourself, "How can I forgive someone who has deeply hurt or wronged me?" Let me start by saying that it's not always easy, but bitterness will grow if unforgiveness is not addressed. We will find ourselves living in a resentful, unhealthy, unsympathetic, and offensive world.

Offense is an intruder that seeks to encroach upon and control our lives. When someone becomes offended and clings to the offense, they cannot live victoriously in Christ. Christ calls us to give our hurts to Him and allow Him to reverse the offense, bringing joy and peace back into our hearts again. This becomes even more challenging when the offending person does not appear to regret it. We may find ourselves filled with anger and dejection; the longer we hold onto our pain, the longer it may take to release it. God has created each of us in His image, filled with love and forgiveness. When we hold onto unforgiveness, it affects us both spiritually and physically. Choosing to seek revenge can lead to anxiety, stress, and depression, and may result in the loss of sleep, increased risk of heart disease, and a weakened immune system. God created us in love, not bitterness.

> "Looking carefully lest anyone fall short of the grace of God; lest any root of bitterness springing up cause trouble, and by this, many become defiled;..." Hebrews 12:15 NKJV

So, how do we forgive? <u>Forgiveness is not necessarily about restoring a relationship with the offender; rather, it is a choice that releases us from being victims</u> of their wrongdoings. Forgiving someone does not mean forgetting the offense; it means acknowledging it and moving forward from the situation.

Forgiveness allows us to release the pain. It's vital to understand that forgiveness is not always instantaneous, as sometimes it comes slowly through perseverance and prayer.

> "He must increase, but I must decrease".
> John 3:30 KJV

> "For those who are living according to the flesh set their minds on the things of the flesh (which gratify the body), but those who are living according to the Spirit, (set their minds on) the things of the Spirit (His will and purpose). Now the mind of the flesh is death (both now and forever-because it pursues sin); but the mind of the Spirit is life and peace (the spiritual well-being that comes from walking with God- both now and forever)" Romans 8:5-6 AMP

In pursuing God's Spirit and His will, we can choose to forgive rather than hold onto revenge. It is not for us to take revenge but to surrender it to God, for He is a just God.

> "If possible, as far as it depends on you, live at peace with everyone. Beloved, never avenge yourselves, but leave the way open for God's wrath (and His judicial righteousness); for it is written (in scripture) 'Vengeance is mine, I will repay,' says the Lord." Romans 12: 18-19 AMP

To forgive, do not focus on how bad the transgression was or what a just solution might be. Instead, concentrate on seeing things from another perspective, empathy. Empathy is the ability to share another person's feelings, which will help you look through the eyes of <u>grace.</u> To do this, I had to realize that the person who hurt me had fallen prey to the adversary.

Many forces of darkness work against us, constantly seeking ways to infiltrate our lives and cause chaos; one of their tactics is to try to damage our relationships. When relationships suffer due to a divorce, it disrupts the entire family and often churches, leading to disunity. Therefore, since that is the enemy's goal, he tries to make the "grass seem greener on the other side," convincing someone to believe a lie. Usually, the victim will slack off from reading God's Word, praying, and attending church regularly, which are the very things that empower Christians, giving them divine insight and the strength to view situations from God's perspective. In essence, the person who hurt us has been misled, or, to put it another way, deceived. When we recognize this, forgiveness becomes more effortless. It does not excuse their actions but allows us to see the enemy's tactics more clearly. When we can adopt this perspective, it becomes easier to forgive. Remember, you are not forgiving them for their sake but so that you can be free.

When I had forgiven, I could pray for the offender–that they would see where they had been deceived and be led toward a transformed life filled with peace. <u>When you can truly pray for someone this way,</u>

<u>you know you have forgiven.</u> In return, I felt free and had a more positive outlook toward others, even outside the relationship.

One of the best illustrations of forgiveness is God's forgiveness toward mankind; He is ready to forgive.

> "Blessed are they whose transgressions are forgiven, whose sins are covered. Blessed is the man whose sin the Lord will never count against him." Romans 4: 7-8 NIV

"We could not work for, or be good enough by our acts in life, to be righteous…" (Huskey, 2019) If God is willing to forgive us of our sins, we should also be willing to forgive others.

> "For if you forgive other people when they sin against you, your heavenly Father will also forgive you." Matthew 6:14 NIV

Forgiveness is not always easy, but forgiveness is essential; once you have forgiven, recovery and making the shift to move forward become much easier.

For further information on offense and forgiveness, go to David Huskey Ministries at <u>www.davidhuskey.org</u>

God can see everything when we cannot.

> "… able to do exceedingly abundantly above all that we ask or think…" Eph 3:20 KJV

So, if He is ABLE to do something, that means He has the ability and the power to do it!

Whether standing on the lawn of a rental property or moving in with family or friends during difficult times, we can emphatically know in our hearts and minds that we are going through the situation victoriously!

[*It's moving day. I try to hold back the tears as I hug the grandchildren goodbye. They have no idea what is happening. I know that things will never be the same when I leave. How does someone my age start over? How do I begin a new life, and what will it look like? My mind spins with questions and confusion.*]

> "Remember ye not the former things, neither consider the things of old. Behold, I will do a new thing; now it shall spring forth…" Isaiah 43: 18-19 KJV

God is doing a NEW work, and it shall spring forth…. Sometimes, it is hard to see it, especially in divorce, but He is working it out. Too often, we sit and think about the things of the past or what life should be like. We want life to be perfected as we see it, and not as God wants to perfect it. He wants our lives to be perfected in Him, and when it is perfected in Him, only then will we be truly happy. Place Him in the driver's seat and become a passenger riding to a new destination.

Self-Help Section

1. I will never leave _____ nor _____ thee.
   Heb 13:5 KJV
2. The Bible states that we are fearfully and _____ made.   Psalms 139:14
3. Who can be against us if _____ is for us? Romans 8:31 KJV
4. God is doing a new _____ in your life. Isaiah 43: 18-19 KJV
5. As I forgive others, God will forgive _____
   Matthew 6: 14
6. I will have perfect _____ if my mind is stayed on God. Isaiah 26:3
7. He must increase, and I must _____ ". John 3:30

I will place my trust in God and allow Him to direct me

___ Yes ___ No ___ Unsure

Notes:
_____
_____

Points to Remember:
1. Unforgiveness is a nasty intruder
2. We can choose to forgive/ change perspective
3. When you can pray for the offender, you know you have forgiven, and inner healing comes faster.
4. God is doing a new work; let Him do the driving, and your life will be perfected in Him.

Prayer for Forgiving Others

Heavenly Father, you know what every person reading this book is going through and their current situation. The wounds often feel as though it is too much to bear. Lord, we ask that You bind and heal the wounds and send comfort during this difficult time. We thank You, Lord, for Your forgiveness and mercy that are freely given to all. We also ask that You help us to forgive others as You have forgiven us. Lord, we ask that You guide, direct, and provide the desired answers for each person to move forward and come out victoriously, serving You. A-Men

DIVORCE MEDICS

8

A New City

[I drive down the roadway, trying to stay strong. My mind is whirling as I prayerfully talk to God about my future. At this point, I let God know I'm willing to go anywhere He wants if He will show me what I'm meant to do. As I reflect on this, the word "Tennessee" flashes into my mind (which I'll discuss later). I pause and think… Tennessee? Where did that come from? It's too cold in Tennessee, so I focus back on my journey.

I'm not sure how I arrived safely at the rental. Even though my family is here to help me with the boxes, I've never felt so alone and desolate. I know God is working on my behalf. Nonetheless, I can still feel the enemy pulling me down, whispering in my ear that I've lost my home and half of my family, that I'm worthless and a disgrace to everyone around me. I keep thinking things will never be the same, that my happiness is gone forever. Even though I know this is exactly what the adversary wants me to believe, it's hard to think of it any other way.]

Individuals going through divorce often have the same thoughts–don't believe this. The Scriptures state that satan is a liar and the father of lies. Push through and resist him!

> "Submit yourselves therefore to God. Resist the devil, and he will flee from you." James 4:7 KJV

Notice it says to first submit to God—this means ceasing to resist and trying to take control. We give it all to God. Then, resist the enemy by putting on the whole armor of God, as stated in Ephesians 6:11-18. Stand equipped with the "helmet of salvation," which protects our minds, and the "breastplate of righteousness," which guards our hearts. Take the "sword of the Spirit, which is the Word of God," in one hand, ready to strike back at the enemy—quote the Word. Put on the "shield of faith" to "quench" the darts the enemy throws. Faith can move mountains! Let your loins be girded with God's truth (the belt of truth, or the good news, around your waist), and your feet strapped with the gospel of peace (standing firm to declare and produce God's goodness). The enemy has no hold! You are mighty in God.

> "… stand still, and see the salvation of the LORD, …" "The LORD shall fight for you, and ye shall hold your peace."
> Exodus 14: 13-14 KJV

All you need to do is stand and watch the Lord. When the enemy comes, the Lord will fight for us. Zechariah 3 tells of the high priest before the angel of the Lord, and guess who stands on the other side? The adversary (satan) himself is ready to oppose him. But the Word tells us that the Lord Himself rebuked the devil.

> "… the high priest standing before the angel of the LORD, and satan standing at his right hand to resist (or accuse) him. And the LORD said unto satan, the LORD rebuke thee…" Zechariah 3:1-2 KJV

Stand on the battlefield equipped, and the Lord will send the enemy running. So, when the adversary places discouragement and confusion into our minds, remember that he is a liar and the father of lies.

> "… there is no truth in him. When he speaketh a lie, he speaketh of his own: for he is a liar, and the father of it."
> John 8:44

Jesus stated that:

"The thief cometh not, but for to steal, and to kill, and to destroy: I am come that they might have life, and that they might have it more abundantly." John 10:10 KJV "and we know that for <u>those who love God all things work together for good, for those who are called according to His purpose."</u> Romans 8:28

Remember these scriptures and quote them when the enemy tries to come in. Don't even give him a toehold—slam the door in his face! No matter what you're going through, if you believe in Christ, these promises hold—cling to them.

[It's a hot August morning, and I'm settling into the rental, unpacking boxes. I start my new job on Monday and will reside in this rental until God changes things. A very long, tearful day has now passed. It's 11:30 pm, and like many others, I lie in bed, staring at the ceiling, wondering how I ended up here.
With so many adjustments, it's hard to get a good night's sleep. I try everything from earplugs and melatonin to even counting sheep. Fumbling for the alarm, I realize I've just dozed off. Therefore, my workdays are fueled by energy shots or sips of caffeine. At night, nothing works—I drift in and out of sleep until one evening... I realize the most powerful answer—as stated earlier... prayer!]

If you remember nothing else from this book, remember that prayer is your most dynamic tool in everything you're going through:

- <u>Prayer helps the weak:</u> Even when we do not know what to pray for or how to pray, the Bible lets us know that in our weaknesses, the Spirit itself intercedes for us.

"… we do not know what prayer to offer or how to offer it as we should, but the Spirit Himself intercedes on our behalf with sighs and groanings too deep for words." Romans 8:26 AMP

- <u>Prayer gives direction:</u> Through prayer, commit to Him, and He will direct you.

"In all thy ways acknowledge Him, and He shall direct thy paths." Proverbs 3:6 KJV

- <u>Prayer gives answers</u> in the most challenging circumstances. Consider Hannah; she bitterly wept before the Lord for a child, as she could not conceive, and yet she had a son.

"… she gave birth to a son…" 1 Samuel 1:20 KJV

How about Paul and Silas? They were thrown into a stinky jail, unsure of what to do. But around midnight, they began to praise God. Then, a great earthquake shook the prison, and the doors flew open; they literally walked out. When we need an answer or a miracle, He has it!

"… and suddenly there was a great earthquake, so that the foundations of the prison were shaken; and immediately all the doors were opened, and everyone's bands were loosed." Acts 16:26 KJV

- <u>Prayer releases anxiety:</u> Only God can give you true peace through stress and hardships. Jesus told us that He would provide us with this true tranquility

"Peace I leave with you, my peace I give unto you; not as the world giveth, give I unto you. Let not your heart be troubled, neither let it be afraid." John 14:27 KJV

Christ gave us this promise so we can trust him for peace of mind.

"Cast all your care upon Him; for He careth for you." 1Peter 5:8 KJV

- <u>Prayer changes the heart</u>: Prayer truly changes things.

"The Lord your God will circumcise your heart and the heart of your descendants to love the Lord your God with all your heart and with all your soul that you may live!" Deuteronomy 30:6 NKJV

God gives us life, not just any life, but He wants to provide us with the "good life." He wants to give us the desires of our hearts!

> "Ask and it will be given to you; seek and you will find; knock and it will be opened to you." Matthew 7:7 NKJV

Matthew continues that if we, with our sinful nature, know how to give good gifts to our children, how much more will our perfect heavenly Father give to those who ask?

<u>Prayer can help you sleep</u>: Prayers calm the spirit and lift the burdens from our day.

> "Come to me, all you who are weary and burdened, and I will give you rest." Matthew 11:28 NIV

> "In peace I will lie down and sleep, for you alone, Lord, make me dwell in safety." Psalms 4:8 NIV

> "Don't worry about anything; instead, pray about everything. Tell God what you need and thank Him for all He has done." Philippians 4:6 NLT

Going a step further, thank Him for what He will do!

> "... The effectual fervent prayer of a righteous man availeth much." James 5:16 KJV

PRAYER IS POWERFUL!

I could go on and on about the various times when God performed miraculous works in response to prayer. <u>Try not to look at the problems, but look to God. He is a problem solver.</u>

> "Fear not, for I am with you; Be not dismayed, for I am your God. I will strengthen you, Yes, I will help you…" Isaiah 41:10 NKJV

When I began praying at night, I could fall asleep faster. Prayer will keep the enemy at bay from bombarding you at night, as he hates prayer.

> "You will keep him in perfect peace whose mind is stayed on you because he trusts in you." Isaiah 26:3 NKJV

Self-Help Section

1. _____ is a liar and the father of all lies.

2. Resist the enemy by putting on the whole _____ of God
Eph 6: 1-18

3. _____ is the most dynamic tool! (It is powerful!)

4. God wants to give us "The good life."

   _____ T _____ F

5. The enemy hates _____

Notes:
_____
_____
_____

Points to Remember:

1. Resist the devil, and he will leave

2. Stand your ground in Christ, and the Lord will fight the battle

3. Prayer is your most dynamic tool

Prayer:

Heavenly Father, I lift up each person as they navigate new beginnings and transitions in their lives. Whether they are relocating to a new city or settling into a different home, grant them the faith to trust in your divine plan. We believe in your Word that everything will be worked out for their good. Thank you for your steadfast guidance and abundant blessings.

In Jesus Name
A-Men

DIVORCE MEDICS

9

Stage 5 Depression/ Sadness:

This is one of the most complex stages, if not the hardest. I recall a time in my life when I felt like happiness would never return, and I just wanted to give up.

[*It's 7 pm, and another 13-hour shift is ending. I am too tired to cook again tonight; my eating habits are far from ideal. I continue to lose weight, lingering around 101-102 lbs. As a nurse, I understand the importance of maintaining proper nutrition during this time, so I begin planning and making adjustments to my diet.*
(which I cover in Chapter 13).

The next few months passed in a blur, with my time spent either working or staying home. Since most of my family and friends are married, and I don't want to be a burden or face constant reminders of my situation, I have chosen solitude for now. I hold onto fleeting moments of hope, wishing my spouse would change his mind and admit he made a huge mistake, but this is not happening. I want my life to return to normal, but I know this is my new normal.

When I look around, the changes in my life feel almost unbearable. I cry when I wake up, go to bed, and cry during the day. I have no desire to do anything; my children are the only reason I care to exist. I often ask myself, "Is it worth it all?" As I walk into the dark parking lot alone, I feel no fear, thinking that if someone took my life, it would just end the pain and misery. But as I reach for the car, the Spirit of God quickens me. I realize the enemy is trying to use these thoughts against me and that I must resist these thoughts because God has a plan for my life.]

It's easy to relive the hurt repeatedly, focusing on the past instead of living in the present. But I wasn't alone, and neither are you.

Connor stated:

"I just sit and think, I mean, there is nothing else to do."

Emily shared:

"I often break down."

John shared:

"I just sat on the floor, rolled up in a ball, and cried for hours."

Danny's story:

Danny and his wife were very fortunate and had been married for years. His wife began working outside the home and grew increasingly dissatisfied with their marriage. They agreed to attend counseling, but her discontent continued. Despite Danny offering more counseling, making changes to benefit her, and both of them acknowledging Biblical principles, she still wasn't happy and insisted on divorce. After countless hours of reviewing legal files and consulting with lawyers, Danny reached a point where he was ready to give up. He had moved to a frame of mind where the situation was now controlling him. One day, during a conversation with a friend, Danny said he could no longer continue. His friend reminded him of the Scriptures:

"I can do all things through Christ, who strengthens me."
Philippians 4:13. NKJV

Danny immediately realized the enemy's tactics and the hopelessness that had overtaken him. He knew that trusting in God was the only way forward. With God on his side, he would emerge victorious if he kept pressing onward.

I share these stories because these feelings are not uncommon and can be overwhelming. It's a time when you face all the fears from the bargaining stage, which can feel suffocating. During this period, there is often no clear plan and little energy to make one. Many people frequently want the time to pass, and some may turn to unhealthy coping mechanisms to ease their pain. Even some of the strongest Christians, in their desperation, have turned to alcohol or drugs during this time because it's hard to face the feelings of loss and being without a partner. However, these self-medications are depressants, which only deepen the emotional turmoil, creating a vicious cycle of despair and isolation.

During this time, we are constantly battling spiritual warfare.

The enemy wants to keep us in guilt, grief, and depression. While depression looks different for each person, it's normal to experience short-term grief, sadness, and even mild depression, but these feelings should not last indefinitely. They should begin to subside in a reasonable amount of time. If you're experiencing depression, reach out to someone—a pastor, counselor, or medical professional. One of the primary keys to getting through this season is to keep moving forward and refusing to quit.

Consider keeping a journal. This will help you feel more in control amid life's chaos. You'll gain clarity and perspective by organizing time and reflecting on events.

The most important advice I received during a group discussion was to give it one year, and things in my life would look very different. I couldn't imagine my life changing in a year at the time, but when the year ended, everything had indeed changed; not in how I had planned, but in how God had orchestrated it, which was for my good. I challenge everyone reading this book to accept where you are, give God one year, and see how things can change. Don't stay stuck in the past or focus on what's happening to you; keep moving forward. Every day is a NEW day.

I Accept My Divorce, So Where Is My Depression Coming From?

There can be many causes of depression, such as chaos, low self-esteem, financial difficulties, body image, or feeling awkward about being single again. Often, it's a combination of factors. So, how can I change the situation? The key is to focus on the things you can change.

Positive Changes:

Set Routines:
Establishing routines is crucial in helping you regain control when you feel overwhelmed by feelings of chaos or disorder. A sense of self-control creates emotional stability.

[*"It's now the fall. I smell the crisp autumn air as I walk into the tiny rental. I pour myself a cup of hot tea and settle into my chair like I do at the end of every day. Bandit, my dog, looks up at me with his big brown eyes, waiting for me to motion for him to come and sit; there is a peaceful silence as the outside world fades away and we enjoy the moment."*]

I knew having a routine would be an essential part of my plan for normalcy. Therefore, I always went to work and rewarded myself with a cup of hot tea when I got home to unwind. My routines would slowly expand as I began to go out briefly on weekends, giving me less time to dwell on negative thoughts. Weekends found me walking my dog at the park, shopping, or having lunch with a friend. I had to get creative and try things I hadn't been able to do in years. This may not be easy at first, but with effort, you will discover new meaning in your life.

Get determined to let go of the past and embrace the present. Your journey may seem long, but when you feel alone in the darkest times, remember—you have a Heavenly Father who is always on your side!

> "The Lord is on my side; I will not fear, ..."
> Psalms 118: 6 NKJV

> "For I know the thoughts that I think toward you, saith the Lord, thoughts of peace, and not of evil, to give you an expected end" Jeremiah 29:11 KJV

> "With God we will triumph...." Psalms 108:13 CEB

Focus on Positive Things:

> "For as he thinks in his heart, so is he"
> Proverbs 23:7 NKJV

If you constantly think about negative things, those negative things will begin to grow and take root in your heart, affecting how you see the world around you. Negative thinking is not uncommon in divorce, but if continued, it will grow and keep you trapped in a negative cycle, which can lead to a feeling of hopelessness. However, positive thinking leads to positive emotions, freeing one from the bondage of negativism, enhancing strength, and paving the way for a brighter future.

Self-Image:

Boost your self-confidence! There's nothing wrong with tooting your own horn. Look at yourself in the mirror and recognize that you are a wonderful person, beautifully made by God. Say that to yourself every day.

It is not humanity or the past that defines you, but God does. What creates the feeling of insignificance is the identity you assign to yourself based on your past, which is not rooted in Christ or how He views you. True significance comes from who you are in Christ as a child of God. Your value is in Him and serving Him. God's Word describes you as precious jewels. Man cannot create a genuine ruby or diamond; they are only created by God and are rare and valuable. This is how your Heavenly Father sees you!

"… For they are like the (precious) jewels of a crown,
Displayed and glittering in His land." Zechariah 9:16 AMP

"…. But not a single sparrow can fall to the ground without your Father knowing it. And the very hairs on your head are all numbered. So, don't be afraid; you are more valuable to God than a whole flock of sparrows." Matthew 10: 29- 31 NLT

"But ye are a chosen generation, a royal priesthood, an holy nation, a peculiar people; …" 1Peter 2:9 KJV

Focus on who you are in Christ. You are awesomely made with a Heavenly identity. So, get out of the house with new friends, have fun, and walk the dog!

Self-Help Section

1. Christians are constantly battling _____ _____.
2. The main "game changer" is to focus on the things that _____ _____ _____.
3. I can do all things through_____ who strengthens me."
   Philippians 4:13
4. Keeping a _____ makes one feel more in control.
5. It is not humanity or the _____ that defines us.
6. God's Word describes me as a precious _____.
7. I am _____ made!

NOTES:
_____

Points to Remember:

1. Live in the present

2. We battle spiritual warfare/ you are a winner with Christ

3. Focusing on positive things and making positive changes gives positive results

4. Accepting where you are brings change/ give God one year

PRAYER

Heavenly Father, I know that you are always with me, no matter what I face in life, and that you are in control. Therefore, I bring all of my burdens, hurts, inadequate feelings, and loneliness, and give them all to you. I know that it is you who defines me and not my situation. I bind the enemy that is trying to control and come against me, every spirit of depression, loneliness, hurt, and low self-esteem; I cast them away through the name of Jesus; you must flee now. I replace all negativity with the love of God, and I command joy, confidence, and peace to come into my life. Lord Jesus, I trust you for complete healing and claim victory in Jesus' name. A-Men

> "…Hope in God and wait expectantly for Him, for I shall yet praise Him, who is the help of my countenance, and my God." Psalms 42:11 AMPC

DIVORCE MEDICS

10

Surviving the Holidays:

[It's now the end of November, and Christmas is almost here. I ponder– "I just want it all to disappear." I sit looking at a tiny Charlie Brown Christmas tree strategically placed on the table because my large tree won't fit in this tiny rental. I've shed too many tears, knowing this year will be different. I feel I've lost half of my family, and this is the hardest thing I've ever been through. No one should have to experience this. I managed to make it through Thanksgiving, but perhaps I should consider getting on a plane and leaving for the remainder of the season. However, since my family expects me to be here, I stay.]

The Holidays

Surviving the holidays; I won't lie, I was resentful and hurt and wanted to crawl under a rock! The holidays are when most people going through a divorce want to escape by planning a trip to avoid family and the whole season. But before you lift that rock to crawl under or run out to buy that plane ticket, here are a few tips:

1. Stop Feeling Guilty! Most people want to avoid others during the holidays because, deep down, they feel guilty that their marriage ended. They think it's because of something they did or because they could have done more to save it. Every marriage faces challenges, and everyone should take responsibility for their mistakes. Everyone makes mistakes; if someone chooses not to work through those difficulties and takes the way out, that was their choice. I went through all the feelings of guilt, trying for months to reconcile. I begged and pleaded, but it was to no avail. If you're like most people reading this book, you didn't want your divorce to happen, and you did everything you could to save your marriage. Please don't feel guilty or take responsibility for their actions. If our Heavenly Father doesn't hold us guilty, then we shouldn't feel guilty.

"But if the unbelieving partner leaves, let him (or her) leave. In such cases, the (remaining) brother or sister is not (spiritually or morally) bound. But God has called us to peace." 1 Corinthians 7:15 AMP

2. Hold Your Head UP!

Don't let anyone drag you down to the point where you think you need to hide from others. You have every right to attend holiday functions with your head held high. Cast off all negativity and turn your head away from antagonistic individuals. If the topic of divorce comes up and you're not ready to talk about it, respond, "I would just rather not talk about it today." The situation is under your control. However, if you feel overwhelmed and would rather stay home, allow yourself the time to heal and politely refuse the invitations; look to your future with great expectations. There will be fantastic holidays ahead.

3. Gifts/ Worrying

You don't need to buy a gift for everyone. Many people try to maintain the same lifestyle before getting divorced, but this is usually impossible. You must accept that changes will occur, and you may be unable to do everything you once did. If you have children, they should be your top priority. If funds are tight, remember that your children will enjoy spending time with you more than anything. If they're old enough, discuss the changes with them and create new holiday traditions. Create lasting memories by baking cookies, playing games, or exploring other ways to bond. Know that God will take care of the rest. Don't worry; trust God. I remember my son asked for designer clothing one Christmas, and I didn't want to disappoint him. I began praying and shopping at second-hand stores. As I sifted through the racks, I found a designer shirt I thought he would love. It still had the tags on it! It had never been worn. I bought it at a fraction of the cost of a new one. Wow! If God can do that for me, He can certainly do it for you! Right then, I knew He cared for me and my children, and everything would be okay. God cares about you, your family, your needs, and, yes, your wants.

"But if God so clothes the grass of the field, which is alive and green today and tomorrow is thrown (as fuel) into the furnace, will He not much more clothe you? You of little faith! Therefore, do not worry or be anxious, saying, 'What are we going to eat?' or 'What are we going to wear?' For the (pagan) Gentiles eagerly seek all things; (but do not worry) for your heavenly Father knows that you need them. But first and most importantly, seek (aim at, strive after) His kingdom and His righteousness (His way of doing and being right- the attitude and character of God), and all these things will be given to you also." Matthew 6: 30-33 AMP

If funds are tight, consider having the kids make the family gifts and attach a card. Most people love receiving such thoughtful, personal gifts. If buying cards isn't in your budget, write them yourself. Most people already have too much stuff, anyway. For neighbors and friends, try baking cookies and packaging them on a paper plate wrapped in red or green cellophane. Get creative! The holidays are about relationships, not material things. It's not about what you have or how much you can give, but about celebrating our Savior's birth, spending time with family, and the love that you share.

4. Stay Busy

Loneliness is one of the biggest challenges during the holidays. It's easy to sit and reminisce, but put the ghost of Christmas past behind you and start new traditions. Focus on others and what you can do to help them. Many churches offer community services, such as toy donations for underprivileged children, food pantries, and cooking and serving meals at homeless shelters. You and your family can volunteer for or participate in many of these activities. Here are a few suggestions:

- Get involved in the local church's play/ choir/ or children's church
- Assist neighbors in cleaning their yards or repairing their homes
- Make holiday gifts for those who are shut-in
- Visit the nursing home and offer to read to them or sit and chat
- Take an elderly person to the grocery or shopping

- Get involved with the local animal shelter
- Volunteer at the veterinary clinic
- Be a temporary foster parent for a pet
- Take homeless children holiday gifts/clothes, or help them have a fun day
- Give the homeless blankets

The most important thing is to stay active, as it helps you feel more emotionally stabilized. Some people join a gym to focus and relieve frustration. Others turn to crafts. I found myself becoming more crafty during this time, creating flower arrangements, scrapbooking, and other projects. Photography is a great hobby, and with the built-in cameras on cell phones today, you don't need to invest a lot of money. Think about all the hobbies you've always wanted to try but never had the time for. Whatever it is, go for it!

5. Juggling the Kids

I know every situation is different, and only you truly know yours. However, in most divorce situations, two caring parents who love their children want to remain a part of their lives. So, whatever you do, do NOT be tempted to work against your ex when scheduling visits during the season. Be willing to give a little. Your ex may have the kids on Christmas Day, but you'll have them the following Christmas. You can celebrate Christmas with the kids earlier;

perhaps have them that morning, and then your ex can spend the evening with them. Consider doing the same with Thanksgiving and other holidays—just be willing to compromise. The children love both of their parents and want to see each one if possible.

You might also want to allow the children to buy a gift for the other parent. It brings them joy and is a small gesture that can make a big difference. I know it's tough, but try to work together and maintain peace.

"Blessed are the peacemakers: for they shall be called the children of God" Matthew 5: 9 KJV

Try to send the children off with a smile, even if you feel like crying. The goal is to let them be happy, even when you may not be. When they return home, try not to be judgmental or ask a thousand questions about what happened while they were gone. Just allow them to share their joy as they wish and talk about how great it was, even if you disagree. Children will feel more comfortable sharing if they believe their parents aren't arguing or harboring ill will toward each other. When children live in environments where there is constant contention between parents, it often increases their anxiety and creates hurtful memories, especially during the holidays. It's hard, I know, because when going through a divorce, we frequently focus on how the holidays are spoiled. But we don't want to sabotage the holidays for them. If you seek peace and strive to be peaceful, you will, in return, bring about peace. Again, do not dwell on the past. Instead, think of beneficial things, which brings us to #6.

6. Have Time to Pray/ Refocus

Take some quiet time to focus on yourself and the positive aspects of life. Spend time with the Lord to ask yourself, " Where do I go from here?" God gives us many answers in quiet times, but you must be willing to slow down to include Him daily in this phase of your life.

> "The effectual fervent prayer of a righteous man availeth much" James 5:16 KJV

Focus on what you want to accomplish as an individual. What can you do to make those things happen? Is it more education or taking on a new job? Whatever it is, start planning how to make it a reality. However, don't try to multitask by setting too many goals in your current life. Just set 1-3 goals to work toward, with only one being a primary goal. Having too many goals can lead to chaos. For example, it would be impossible to write a book, start a new job, take care of your children, learn a new language, and travel the world, though all of these might be things you want to do, they may not be practical. More realistic goals might include starting a new job (your primary goal), going to the gym twice a week, and keeping a daily journal.

7. Relax:

Do the things that make you happy. Treat yourself to a massage, a walk, or something relaxing just for you. When you relax, your blood pressure, heart rate, and hormone levels return to normal. Relaxation will enable you to sleep better and cope with stressful situations more effectively. Go ahead—have a cup of tea, turn up the music, and dance!

Self-Help Section

1. I will not allow myself to feel guilty or take responsibility for their _____.
2. I will throw off negativity and turn my head away from _____ individuals.
3. God has called us to _____. 1 Corinthians 7:15 AMP
4. I don't have to buy a gift for everyone.   True _____ or False _____
5. One of the biggest challenges during the holidays is _____.
6. One key to Loneliness is to stay _____. Matthew 5:9 KJV
7. It is in the quiet times that God will give us many _____.
8. "… seek first the kingdom of God and all these things will be added unto _____. Matthew 6:30-33 AMP
9. "The effectual fervent prayer of a _____ _____ availeth much." James 5:16

Points to Remember:
1. Stop feeling guilty
2. It is not the Gift that is important
3. Stay busy and do things that bring joy
4. Hold your head up/ pray
5. Learn to Relax

Heavenly Father,

During this holiday season, I lift up all who are navigating the pain of divorce, and those feeling sad and lonely. Bring light into their darkest corners and remind them that they are never truly alone. Bring them moments of joy, peace, and a new beginning they did not expect. Help them find strength in each day and hope in what is yet to come, and lead them toward healing with Your love. A-men

DIVORCE MEDICS

11

Recovery Stage/ Making the shift

[*It has now been months. Some days, I feel like I have a handle on things; other days, I collapse because it still feels like a dream. As I walk into work one morning, a co-worker asks me, "How are things going?" I break down, sharing how things are in my life. Despite some time having passed, I'm still, at times, an emotional wreck. She advises me to get help, and we discuss a divorce support group she had attended that she thinks could help me. Though I'm reluctant, I realize I'm an emotional mess, and maybe this is God's direction for me, so I decided to attend.*

It's late Thursday, and I've found the support group. Pulling into the parking lot, I'm unsure whether to go inside or run. What are their stories? Will they all be younger than me, making me the "older" one in the group? Will this even help me, or am I just wasting my time? How many people my age even get divorced? I feel embarrassed and alone.]

As written in the preface of this book, divorce doesn't isolate anyone. There are over 16,800 divorces per week in the U.S., totaling 876,000 annually (McKinley Irvin Family Law). Many others are going through similar situations. Divorce doesn't just affect younger people—it can happen at any stage in life. It's up to each individual to decide how to change their circumstances and move forward.

[*For me, moving forward meant I had nothing to lose by attending a support group, so I walked in cautiously. I quickly realized that the group's members were of all ages, and no one was judging me. It was a relaxing, empathetic atmosphere. Everyone shared their stories during the meetings, but I remained silent. I came to understand that it was okay to attend without pressure to speak. Over the following weeks, I shared very little, but <u>I realized there are answers and ways to gradually change the circumstances to regain a normal lifestyle</u>. The group also helped me better understand how others had dealt with similar situations. Joining the group was one of my best decisions, and it helped me move out of isolation. There comes a time when everything must change, and one must be determined to make the shift.*]

> "He heals the brokenhearted and binds up their wounds."
> Psalm 147:3 AMP

Making The Shift:

[*It's Sunday morning, and I still battle mixed emotions as I prepare for church. However, I am determined to make a change, to continue attending the support group, and, above all, to trust God. I know I must move forward with my life. As I drive into the church parking lot, I pray, "God, I accept my life as it is; please help me stop crying and get me past this."*

> *"God is our refuge and strength, an ever-present help in trouble." (or need) Psalms 46:1 NIV*

The service begins, and I push past all resistance, knowing that God will turn things around for the good. As I raise my hands to honor God, I can feel the weight on me lift away. I became part of the service, trusting God and participating, no longer just sitting and hoping it would all disappear. When the church service is over, I feel much lighter in my spirit and renewed.]

How did this suddenly happen? <u>Resistance… pushing past the enemy.</u>

> "… when the enemy shall come in like a flood, the Spirit of the LORD shall lift up a standard against him." Isaiah 59: 19 KJV
>
> "For the weapons of our warfare are not carnal, but mighty through God to the pulling down of strong holds;) casting down imaginations, and every high thing that exalteth itself

against the knowledge of God and bringing into captivity every thought to the obedience of Christ;" 2 Corinthians 10: 4-5 KJV

[*When the service ends, I know God has worked something within me. The next day, I woke up early and went to work as usual. It's another hectic Monday where I routinely walk the halls, holding back tears. But not today! I keep it together, and I leave work on time. At home, I dart around, doing chores and preparing dinner. Then, I realize, "I haven't cried today!"*]

I had pushed past the enemy and was determined to give all my cares to the Lord. From that day forward, the tears became less frequent until they ceased altogether. Over the following months, I continued attending church and my support group, while learning how to manage life after divorce more effectively and how to live victoriously.

[*It's early in the week, and after a long day, I sit down to relax when the phone rings. I had applied for a loan to build a new home, but things didn't look promising, as I had only been working at my new job for a short time. However, I continued praying about the situation. I nervously sat and listened to the loan officer, who informed me that I needed to submit additional documents. To my surprise, they were granting me the loan! I'm ready to build! God is good! I spend the evening calling family and friends, rejoicing in God, and contemplating my future.*]

Turn it all over to Jesus! Let go of the negative thoughts that your mind is fixated on. God doesn't have control when you hold onto things, but if you give them to Him, He will work things out. It's not meant for us to stay stuck in the past or live a life of isolation. You may be unable to change the past or your situation, but God can! I once heard it stated:

> "Humpty Dumpty sat on a wall, Humpty Dumpty had a great fall; all the king's horses and all the king's men could not put Humpty together again, ...
>
> (author unknown)

But GOD can!...... He can fix anything!

There is NOTHING that God cannot do! Some of the best advice I received was to dedicate one year of my life to God, and I would see things change. Once I took this advice, I became determined to walk through the doors God was opening for me and to allow things to fall into place in a prayerful manner. This didn't mean I went through the divorce, ignoring reality, with my head stuck in the sand like an ostrich, hoping it would all go away, but it did mean I would pray and be wise in handling legal and financial matters, trusting and leaning on God.

> "Trust in the Lord withal thine heart; and lean not unto thine own understanding." Proverbs 3:5 KJV

I quoted two scriptures almost every day, which encouraged me, and I hope will also be encouraging to you:

> #1 "…All things work together for the good of them that love God…" Romans 8:28 KNV

Note, it says, "all things"—yes, even your current situation. God is the one who can change things and turn them completely around. If you belong to Christ, you have His DNA in you. When you are united with Christ, you are "one Spirit with Him." He is our Heavenly Father and wants to provide for His children and design a better future for us.

> #2 "The steps of a good man are ordered by the Lord…" Psalms 37:23 KJV (This includes us women)

<u>God's children do not aimlessly walk around but are directed by Him, walking in His power.</u>
When life feels broken and hopeless, there is still hope. Devote this year to God, prayerfully hold on to Him, and see what happens.

> "…to give unto them beauty for ashes, the oil of joy for mourning, the garment of praise for the spirit of heaviness." Isaiah 61: 3 KJV

Self-Help Section

1. Trust in the Lord and lean not on your own _____ Proverbs 3: 5-6
2. When the enemy comes in like a _____, the Lord shall lift up a standard. Isaiah 59:19 KJV
3. All things work together for the good of them that _____ ___

   Romans 8:28
4. The steps of a good man (or woman) are ordered ____ ___ _____.

   Psalm 37:23
5. …To give them beauty for _____

   Isaiah 61:3 KJV

I commit to not living a life of regret, but rather to moving forward.

Yes ___ No ___ Unsure

NOTES: _____

Points to Remember:

1. Push past all Resistance from the enemy

2. A support group can be beneficial

3. Walk in God's power

My Prayer for You:

Heavenly Father,

My heart is burdened for those reading through the pages of this book. You know what they are going through and their current situation. Their wounds are deep, and they often feel like it is too much to bear. I ask you, Lord, to bind and heal their wounds and comfort them during this difficult time. I asked, Lord, that you guide, direct, and give them answers to the questions they may have. I command the spirits of depression and sadness to depart from them and to flee, never to return; let it be replaced with peace and joy in their hearts so that they may live a victorious life for you. In Jesus' name, Amen

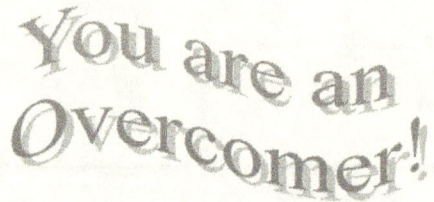

DIVORCE MEDICS

12

Having Significance and Living in Divine Purpose:

To have significance is to recognize one's self-worth or importance. Purpose, on the other hand, is the reason something is done or created. It's the goal or intent. Living for a purpose gives us meaning and importance in life. However, without a sense of purpose, a person may feel that their life lacks significance or self-worth. I know that's a lot to digest, so let's break it down.

After we graduate from high school, and often college, we start planning for the future. We "shoot for the stars" or "plan to set the world on fire." Along the way, we search for the perfect job, house, and partner. We believe that once we have these things, we'll have reached our goals and discovered our true identity. But then, life happens. Our goals don't always unfold as we envisioned, and things become muddled. Indubitably, we feel as though we've lost our significance and purpose. It's as if there's a massive hole in our core.

The truth is that a person will never feel fulfilled entirely until they find their identity in God first. It doesn't matter whether you've been through a divorce or whether you've achieved specific life goals—these things should not define who we are. As discussed earlier in this book, our true identity is found in Christ. There is a place within each person that's reserved only for God. If this spot isn't filled with Christ, we're left feeling devoid or empty and unable to cope with life's pressures. This is why even those with millions of dollars may struggle with addiction or even contemplate suicide. It's like a pot of tea boiling with a lid on it; eventually, it will overflow without a release valve. Every person needs Christ as their safety valve; He becomes our hiding place. Those who don't know Him find it hard to cope with life's pressures because they lack this crucial release. Why is this the case? I'm glad you asked…

Each person, each human, is made up of body, soul, and spirit, all intertwined. Our body is the physical self, made of flesh and bone; our cells, organs, nervous system, head, neck, torso, legs, and feet. <u>Hang with me here</u>… Our soul is our inner being, encompassing our thoughts and reasoning. The Greek word for soul is psyche, and the Hebrew word is nephesh, meaning breath or life. God literally breathed life into mankind. Finally, there is our spirit, which is our connection to God. When we become Christians, believing that Jesus is Lord and our Savior, we find He connects with our spirit and dwells within us.

"For whoever finds me finds life,…" Proverbs 8:35 NKJV

> "… Happy are the people whose God is the Lord"
> Psalms 144: 15 NKJV

Our true happiness comes from within, from the fulfillment only God can provide.

The first step in finding significance is having Christ in our lives; He is the bridge to salvation, to God, and true happiness. Once we fill the gap with Him, God works in our lives, leading us into a life of victory.

> "For as many as are led by the Spirit of God, these are the sons (or daughters) of God." Romans 8:14

How does the Spirit lead us? Through prayer and God's Word. He often gives answers through His Word, which the Bible describes as "a lamp to our feet and a light to our path."

> "… lamp unto my feet and a light unto my path"
> Psalms 119:105 NKJV

How can we see clearly if we don't study His Word? The more we study, the brighter the light becomes, revealing the way forward. In studying His Word, we learn about His grace, His plan for humanity, and our role within it.

> "Adonai directs a person's steps, …"
> Psalms 37: 23 CJB

As God directs our steps, we begin to find our true destination. God is our compass, showing us the way. He speaks to us through His Word, through prayer, or that "still small voice" where His Spirit connects with ours. Hearing Him and following His guidance becomes easier when we walk with Him in a loving relationship.

> "My sheep hear My voice, and I know them, and they follow Me." John 10:27 NKJV

> "I am the Good Shepherd, and I know (without any doubt those who are) My own and My own know Me"
> (and have a deep, personal relationship with Me.)
> John 10:14 AMP

You may feel that your life is broken and shattered, with no hope. But I'm here to tell you there is hope. When we live in our God-directed purpose, true joy and significance are found and will last forever.

> "You make me know the path of life; in your presence is unbounded joy, in your right hand eternal delight."
> Psalms 16:11 CJB

Confirming Your Relationship with Christ

Salvation Scriptures:

"But if from thence thou shalt seek the Lord thy God, thou shalt find Him, if thou seek Him with all thy heart and with all thy soul." Deuteronomy 4:29 KJV

"Jesus said to him, "I am the way, and the truth, and the life. No one comes to the Father except through me." John 14:6 ESV

"…God was manifest in the flesh, … 1 Timothy 3:16 KJV

"…. And they shall call His name Emmanuel, which being interpreted is, God with us." Matthew 1: 23 KJV

"Neither is there salvation in any other; for there is none other name under heaven given among men, whereby we must be saved." Acts 4:12 KJV

"For whoever calls on the name of the Lord shall be saved." Romans 10:13 NKJV

"For God so loved the world that He gave His only begotten Son, that whoever believes in Him should not perish but have everlasting life." John 3:16 NKJV

"that if you confess with your mouth the Lord Jesus and believe in your heart that God has raised Him from the dead, you will be saved. For with the heart one believes unto righteousness, **and with the mouth confession is made unto salvation**. Romans 10:9-10 NKJV

PRAYER FOR SALVATION:

Heavenly Father, I come before You now, fully surrendering and seeking a complete transformation. I believe that Jesus Christ is my Lord and Savior, that He died for my sins, and through His death, burial, and resurrection, I am forgiven. Your Word says, "For whoever calls on the name of the Lord shall be saved." I claim that promise today that my spirit (the real you) will be reborn unto God, my Heavenly Father. I invite you into my heart to rule and reign so that your perfect will may be fulfilled in my life. Guide me through Your Holy Spirit and help me grow in the knowledge of who You are to receive all You have for me. I am thankful, Lord, for the gift of salvation.   A-Men.

If you are not currently connected with a local church, I encourage you to find one where you will feel at home, study God's Word, and be water baptized. Water baptism represents Christ's death, burial, and resurrection and is a public display of this. Christ was baptized, as an example for us to follow. (The blood of Christ is what cleanses us from sin) Being part of a church community where you have friends you can walk with, grow with, and lean on when things get tough. I know it has made a big difference for me, and I'd love for you to experience that too.

13

Health and Nutrition

You may remember the commercial that said, "You are what you eat, from your head down to your feet," or maybe it's new to you. Regardless, it holds a lot of truth! The quality of our nutrition affects our resistance to diseases and plays a key role in maintaining good health. So, how do we ensure that we get the proper nutrients when we're focused on other matters or unable to eat?

When I was navigating through a difficult divorce, I lost a lot of weight, so much so that I began to worry about my health. (We will discuss weight gain later) As an RN, I knew I needed to devise a plan to combat this matter. I know... this is easier said than done when you're struggling to eat. However, focusing on consuming small meals and gradually increasing your intake can help you manage your diet and maintain your weight. And yes, I understand—many people are happy to lose weight, but this is not a good way to do so, and you don't want to put yourself at risk. Additionally, good nutrition plays a significant role in mental clarity, and during a divorce, it is essential to stay focused.

Some ideas for small meals may include:

1. A small amount of oatmeal with fruit or toast with egg and fruit.
2. Yogurt and fruit.
3. Egg muffin with spinach, bell peppers, and onions; bake in the oven until set for an easy grab-and-go meal.
4. Tuna salad wraps
5. Soup and sandwich
6. A protein smoothie drink
7. Pan-seared salmon with kale and spinach
8. Stir-fry with rice and veggies (add your choice of meats)

I could go on. The primary objective is to balance protein, carbohydrates, and fats throughout the day. Try to aim for around 40% carbohydrates, 30% protein, and 20% fats. Carbohydrates and fats typically come easily, but protein intake can be challenging for many, especially those who follow a vegan or vegetarian diet. I was no different.

As I researched protein sources, I discovered that eggs are one of the richest sources of protein. Just three tablespoons of egg whites contain about 5 grams of protein and can be added to many recipes. I also learned that ½ cup of lentils provides 12 grams of protein, kidney beans offer 7 grams, and peas have 4 grams. For those who eat meat, a chicken breast contains about 56 grams, and a slice of roast beef offers around 22 grams; you get the idea.

Incorporating these protein-rich foods into your diet is a great start, especially if your goal is to improve your overall health. Adding supplements may be necessary to reach your nutrition goals.

There are several ways to fill any nutritional gaps. One option is to incorporate over-the-counter vitamins and minerals. However, I would caution against adding supplements without consulting your healthcare provider first, as they can interact with other medications. Always consult with your healthcare provider before starting any new supplements. You may also want to explore the many flavorful and nutritious shakes available. All vitamins and minerals play a role in our health, but here are a few that I consider especially important:

1. Vitamin C - When stressed, you are more prone to illness and disease. Vitamin C boosts your immune system, thereby helping protect you from sickness. It also helps synthesize neurotransmitters, such as serotonin, which regulates our mood, and norepinephrine, which is involved in the stress response. Vitamin C is found in broccoli, citrus fruits, and other vegetables; however, individuals usually do not get enough. Thus, this is where supplements come in.

2. Vitamin B12- Involved in RBC (Red blood cell) formation, which carries oxygen to our organs and helps to protect our nerves. It is also involved in our metabolism and energy levels. Note: Take vitamin B12, but wait at least 2 hours before taking vitamin C, as it may interfere with its absorption. Additionally, taking other

supplements, such as vitamin B, may be beneficial, so it's a good idea to check these as well.

3. Vitamin D- It is essential for bone health, inflammation in the body, mood, etc. It can be found in milk, cereals, orange juice, and foods fortified with vitamin D.
4. Omega-3s are essential for maintaining brain and heart health, as well

    as reducing inflammation, among other benefits. It is found in fish,

    such as tuna, as well as in walnuts, flaxseed, and Brussels sprouts.
5. Calcium- Good for bone, muscle, nerve transmission, etc. It is found in milk, yogurt, cheese, broccoli, and kale, among other foods. This mineral usually needs to be supplemented, especially in women.
6. Vitamin K- It supports bone health and blood clotting. (Consult your Medical Provider <u>before beginning</u> <u>vitamin K,</u> as it may interfere with medications, and honestly, not one that I take every day, as it can thin the blood.) It is found in kale, spinach, dark leafy vegetables, broccoli, and beef liver. (Although not my forte, liver is good for you.)
7. Multi-Vitamins- A multi-vitamin will help to "fill in the gaps" for vitamins to ensure you are not missing out on the essential ones. However, no supplement can replace the benefits of a well-balanced diet.

<u>Contact your healthcare provider with concerns or questions about your medications or when beginning supplements.</u> If you're

experiencing ongoing weight loss or difficulty eating, it may be helpful to consult a nutritionist in addition to your provider, who can offer a more comprehensive approach to your health.

Weight Gain:

Weight gain during and after divorce is not unusual, and it can stem from lifestyle changes and emotional stress. It is because one of the most common coping mechanisms is "comfort foods." These comfort foods are a way of coping with stress, anxiety, loneliness, and or depression. These foods are typically high in sugar, fat, or carbohydrates, offering temporary relief but often leading to weight gain. Although they may bring momentary satisfaction, the high sugar, carb, and calorie content only contributes to further weight gain. This can become a pattern that is hard to break. It is always better to seek out solutions that will lead you to better health.

Another reason for weight gain is eating out. Some individuals would prefer to eat out rather than cook for themselves. Foods typically prepared in restaurants are higher in sugar, carbs, calories, and fats, and the proportions are more significant than when dining at home, making it harder to maintain a healthy weight.

Finally, weight gain could be attributed to stress; yes, that's right, stress. This is the same cortisol released in the fight-or-flight mechanism discussed earlier in the book. When stressed, our body releases cortisol; this increase in cortisol can cause a person to feel hungry, thereby increasing the need to eat and contributing to weight gain. Prolonged cortisol levels and weight gain can also increase the risk for heart disease, along with other health issues.

The journey to good health is about progressing one step at a time. The path to wellness is about listening to your body and making mindful choices.

Budgeting/ Finances

14

Being a Good Steward/ Finances:

[It's now the end of February, and God has blessed me with a home. When everything is unpacked, I look around at my humble beginnings. My living room has one TV, a small sofa, a plant stand, and a candle holder. I have no end tables, lamps, rugs, drapes, or anything on the walls. As I entered the kitchen, I saw that I only had the essential appliances and utensils. Glancing into the dining room, it's empty. This will take time and a miracle, but I am thankful that God will continue to bless and guide me.]

After a divorce, living on one income can become quite challenging. While most people recognize the need for a budget, they often don't follow through. Instead, they'll cut back on some conveniences and try to track their expenses mentally. While this may work temporarily, it doesn't provide a clear picture of your financial situation. When you're working full-time, dealing with car repairs, the kids are crying, cooking every meal, laundry is piling up due to a broken dryer, and you can't afford help, the story changes. Even though budgeting takes time and effort, it helps ensure bills are paid and needs are met. Without a financial outline, you risk mismanaging your hard-earned money and inviting unnecessary stress. God's Word reminds us to manage our finances wisely.

> "Show yourself in all respects to be a model of good works, and in your teaching show integrity, dignity" Titus 2:7 ESV

> "And the Lord said, Who then is that faithful and wise steward, whom his lord shall make ruler over his household, to give them their portion of meat in due season?" "Blessed is that servant, whom his lord when he cometh shall find so doing when he comes." Luke 12: 42-43 KJV

Some people see budgeting as a form of confinement; in reality, it offers freedom. Tracking your cash flow can bring financial liberty, allowing you to avoid financial stress. In return, you'll be able to establish a more comfortable and manageable lifestyle. Money, money, money ...

This does not mean you should put all your faith in your budget or its potential wealth. God hasn't designed us to put our faith in our finances, but to trust Him.

> Jesus stated, "Lay not up for yourselves treasures upon earth, where moth and rust doth corrupt, and where thieves break through and steal: But lay up for yourselves treasures in heaven, where neither moth nor rust doth corrupt, and where thieves do not break through nor steal: For where your treasure is there will your heart be also." Matthew 6: 19-21 KJV

> "… If riches increase, do not set your heart on them". Psalm 62: 10 NKJV

In other words, we shouldn't set our hearts on wealth. Instead, we should rely on wisdom and trust in God, knowing He will bless us with increase. While financial wisdom is crucial, we should not let money control us.

At the same time, it's natural to want to avoid poverty, and it's not God's intention for us to live in hardship. By budgeting wisely, we can steer clear of financial missteps and receive God's blessings.

> "He who is of a proud heart stirs up strife, but he who trusts in the Lord will be prospered." Proverbs 28:25 NKJV

> "… those who walk in wisdom are kept safe." Proverbs 28:26 NIV

When we place our trust in God and use wisdom, we can have faith to know He will guide us through every situation, and we will prosper. This doesn't mean you'll get everything you desire, but your needs will be met when you follow Christ.

When my oldest son was about 7, he wanted a new pair of shoes. We were on a very tight budget that year, and I reluctantly told him he would have to wait. But he was persistent. So, I said, "Unless the shoes are $3.50, you'll need to wait." When we went to the store, he rushed to the shoe department and returned with the cutest white tennis shoes. In my carnal thinking, I thought, "Oh boy, these are going to cost a fortune," but when he showed them to me, to my amazement, they were priced at exactly $3.50! God often reminds us of His provisions and love for us in such times like these. Let it be known: God cares about everything—your children, your home, and yes, your finances. Do your part, trust in Him, and it will work out.

> "Trust in Him at all times; ye people, pour out your heart before Him; God is a refuge for us" Psalms 62:8 NKJV

God is a strong tower, our rock, our protector, and our provider! His Word is truth and will not fail.

> "The name of the Lord is a strong tower; the righteous run to it, and are safe." Proverbs 18:10 NKJV

> "The Lord is my rock, and my fortress, and my deliverer; my God, my strength, in whom I will trust; my buckler, and the horn of my salvation, and my high tower." Psalms 18:2 KJV

A tower is high, strong, and usually made of brick. It's a place of safety and can offer protection from the enemy. When you're in the tower, you can see the enemy approaching and prepare for the attack. We can place our trust in God, knowing He is our tower, and when attacks come, we can run to Him for refuge. So, when the enemy attacks your finances and you're struggling, place your faith in God and plan for victory through Christ. Do your part— plan and budget as you should, and He will do His.

Setting up a Budget

You must first lay out all your expenses to create a financial plan. I like to think of it as a financial blueprint. A blueprint is carefully drawn and followed to achieve the desired result for a project. This blueprint can be modified as needed. A budget is the same: lay everything out and create a monthly plan. I have given an example of a simple strategy and budget plan on the following pages.

1. Set the foundation by writing your core goals.

    A. What are your goals? Think about both short- and long-term goals; what do you need to pay off first, how much do you need to put in savings, or what are your most significant expenses? Vacation? Saving for a down payment on a home or a retirement fund?

2. Establish the outline or framework and create the budget.

The Framework or Budget Plan:

    A. How do you get paid? Weekly/bi-weekly/ monthly?

    B. What is your income?

    C. Do you receive bonuses?

    D. What are your debts? (This is everything: your groceries, mortgage, utilities, insurance payments, childcare, loans, credit cards, even the gas you need for that time in your car)

    E. What are your credits? (income)

    F. Spending? (include the extras like going to the movies, clothing, etc.)

    G. What is your cushion budget? (This is extra money that you have for emergencies)

3. Adjust: Make the necessary adjustments.

You can follow many different budget designs; therefore, you'll need to find one that suits you best. The following page provides an example of a simple budget plan. If your financial status is more complicated, you may want to seek help from a Certified Public Accountant (CPA) or financial planner.

Simple Budget:

INCOME	DEBITS	CREDITS	OTHER
$ 2,604	TOTAL - $2,335.00	+ $50.00	- $205.00
	MORTGAGE 700.00	BONUS (every mo.) 50.00	CLOTHING 50.00
	POWER 300.00		EAT OUT 50.00
	WATER/ TRASH 55.00		X-TRA 50.00
	CABLE 130.00		SAVINGS 55.00
	GROCERIES 400.00		
	GAS 150.00		
	CAR 230.00		
	INSURANCE 70.00		
	CREDIT 100.00		
	LIFE INS. 35.00		
	MEDICAL 30.00		
	MEDICATIONS 80.00		
	CELL PHONE 55.00		
TOTAL INCOME: $2,654.00	TOTAL $ 2,335.00	TOTAL $50.00 TOTAL DEBITS: $2,540.00	TOTAL $205.00 DIFFERENCE: $114.00

As you can see, there would be a minimal "cushion" at the end of the month based on the debt-to-income ratio, so some adjustments may need to be made in this situation. However, this budget has columns for extra cash. Just remember always to have a "cushion."

Putting Your Budget into Action

Once you have a budget, organize your bills by their due dates and mark them on your calendar accordingly. It may seem trivial, but according to NerdWallet, just over half of adults aged 18-34 pay their bills on time. (Issa, 2016) This doesn't account for those over 34, so we can assume that the percentage is higher. Keeping your monthly payments visible will help prevent missed payments and avoid late fees, penalties, and damage to your credit score.

Tracking Your Finances

Tracking your monthly spending helps you see where your money is going and prevents overspending. It can be tricky if you're busy, and if you're like me, you might prefer the old-fashioned way of keeping receipts and organizing them into categories for spreadsheets. Setting this up takes some time, but it can be worth it. Alternatively, you could track your spending in each category and keep a running total. More advanced tools, such as Excel, and popular apps like Mint, PocketGuard, and Wally, also exist. These apps link directly to your account and allow for customizations. It doesn't matter which method you use, as long as you find one that works for you and stick with it.

LIVING ON A SKINNY BUDGET

[The sun is shining; it's a beautiful day as I plan my future and figure out how to furnish my home. Although I have a good job, I still live on a tight budget, so I am hoping it won't take years to complete my décor. Humm... If I buy most of my furnishings on a credit card, I could get what I need or want, and pay it off later.] That sounded great, except for the fact that when you buy on credit, you pay a fat interest charge every month. Even though I would pay each month on the credit card, I would not decrease my debt because the interest would increase the amount owed. However, some cards state "no interest" for a year, which, my friend, sounds even better.... "No interest" ... Read the fine print! The moment you are a day late, the rate increases to the maximum amount on most cards. So, if you get busy for one month and you forget to pay on time, your reasonable rate is no longer "reasonable." Not to mention, they don't tell you your rate has increased; it just happens.

[The best thing for me to do is to stay within my budget and shop wisely.]

I trusted God and set out for the nearest thrift store. People often rave about them, and while I've visited a few in the past, it was mostly just for fun, not as a serious shopper in need of home furnishings. But now, living on a tight budget, it's time to dive in. Here we go. I walk into a local thrift store, and soon, something catches my eye. There, amid all the dusty items, were two end tables with potential. I knew they would need a little stain, but the price was reasonable, so I walked out with both for $60. What a win! Over the next couple of days, I cleaned and stained them; wow, they looked as good as new! I could get used to this!

On my next shopping adventure, I wanted to purchase two bedside tables, as God had already blessed me with a bedroom set for a little over $ 600. I had a style in mind for the end tables and did not want to spend much on them. I was able to purchase both at a local store for around $100. Thrifty Nifty!

> "The Lord bless thee, and keep thee; The Lord make His face shine upon thee, and be gracious unto thee; The Lord lift up His countenance upon thee, and give thee peace."
> Numbers 6: 24-26

Next stop, the grocery store. Since I was spending money to furnish the home, I prayed that the grocery bill would not be over $100.00. I glanced at the total; it was definitely over $100,00. Then the cashier asked if I had a grocery reward card.

I remembered I had just received one; my total was $99.00!

God is so Good!

> "But my God shall supply all your need according to His riches in glory by Christ Jesus. Now unto God and our Father be glory for ever and ever. Amen."
> Philippians 4: 19-20

Living on a skinny budget does not mean that you must live under harsh circumstances; it can be surprisingly comfortable if you make some adjustments. Visit the Thrift stores, obtain the grocery cards, and clip a few coupons; it's worth it. God will bless you as you!

Skinny Budget Rules to Follow

Stop impulsive buying. Impulsive buying can take many forms, such as emotional impulse buying, fear of missing out on a sale, the last-minute buyer, and what I call the "bored shopper syndrome."

1. Emotional Impulse Buying:
   When someone purchases an item due to an emotional impulse, it's because the individual experiences a
   "high," which is caused by the release of dopamine. Dopamine is a chemical that is transmitted between the nerve cells and activates the pleasure center of the brain. So, when we purchase the product, it temporarily makes us feel happy.

2. The Fear of Missing the Sale:

   This shopper sees a sale and fear takes over, convincing them they'll miss out on the savings if they don't buy immediately. But if we take a moment to think, we know that sales like this will inevitably return. Despite this, shoppers impulsively make the purchase, reassuring themselves that they've made a wise choice by saving money by buying now instead of later.

3. The Last-Minute Buyer:

The last-minute buyer is the type of person who, as they approach the checkout line, their eyes begin to scan everything on display. Eventually, something catches their eye –an item they "must have." After all, it's reasonably priced, so they purchase it right then, as if it might not be there the next time; they go through the checkout. Yep!

4. The Bored Shopper:

The bored shopper is common, especially among divorcees– and I can't say I'm innocent of this myself. When you're single, let's face it: there are times when boredom sets in. So, what do we do? We head to town to get out of the house and escape the endless stare at four walls. Since we have no destination, we begin at the local coffee shop, and thus, the first $5.00 to $10.00 is spent. We then stroll around town on a noble quest to buy anything that sparks joy, boosts dopamine, and tricks our brains into thinking we've accomplished something for the day. Ultimately, we usually do, as we spend $50 to $100 very quickly.

5. Eating out:

There is nothing wrong with eating out, but it can become an expensive habit if done too often. This might be surprising, but you don't have to dine out every week. If you are accustomed to this, try eating out every other week instead, and if you opt for lunch, it usually costs less than eating out during dinner, which is the prime time.

6. Plan Meals:

    Most people hate meal planning, and I can relate. I find it easier to stick to 5-8 enjoyable meals and rotate them. If you're working, a crockpot can be a real lifesaver — it's easy to use, budget-friendly, and has meals ready when you get home.

    If you have a large family, there are many budgetfriendly meal options, such as chicken and rice, peanut butter sandwiches with soup, salads, or simple casseroles. It doesn't need to be a four-course feast to be satisfying.
    When my children were small, I would buy a whole chicken and cut it into two pieces. We would then have fried chicken one night and chicken and rice the other night. You can cut your grocery bill in half by planning your meals.

7. Frugal grocery shopping:

    When grocery shopping, look for coupons to maximize your savings. You can clip coupons from your local newspaper, use apps, or find them online, and your savings can add up quickly. Once you have your coupons, don't hesitate to visit different grocery stores to find the best deals. I would always go to my local store, where they rewarded my loyalty with discounts and points for gas. I'd then head to the discounted market for nonperishables to save even more. Stick to your shopping list and avoid shopping when you're hungry. Stay within your grocery budget, and if necessary, use a calculator as you shop to ensure you don't exceed it. I understand that many people with large families buy in bulk to save money. However, I'd caution that just because there's more of an item doesn't always mean you're saving. Do the math, or you could spend more than you planned.

8. Monitor the Utilities:

Monitoring utilities has never been more straightforward. Some monitoring tools connect to your electrical panel to track your home's energy usage. Some can identify when a light is left on, and you can view all this information through your smartphone. To help save energy, make it a habit to turn off lights when leaving a room. This keeps the room cooler in the summer and reduces energy consumption. The amount you save will depend on the type of bulb you use. For example, a 40-watt bulb costs you about $0.04 per hour.

9. Movie Night:

Although you may have become accustomed to weekly movie outings, switching to monthly trips might be a more budget-friendly option. The matinees are typically cheaper; however, the cost can still add up.

Alternatively, consider hosting in-home movie nights. Redbox offers a wide variety of movies, and you can stream films on

Roku, Netflix, and Amazon for a fraction of the price. You don't have to give up movie night, or, for that matter, anything - just adjust.

As I stated at the beginning of the chapter, I had to start over, but God did many amazing things for me. When I first moved into my home, I had minimal furniture. But within six months, it was fully furnished. I was incredibly blessed and eventually able to purchase a rental house. <u>Never</u> underestimate the power of God, as He loves blessing His children, just as we love blessing ours. God is good!

End Note:

As I expressed earlier in the book, one of my favorite scriptures is: "The steps of a good man are ordered by the Lord..." (or woman) Psalm 37:23 KJV

When I prayed for guidance from God, the words "Tennessee" came into my thoughts very vividly; it was like a flash. I quickly brushed it off, thinking, "My son likes Tennessee. Humm... It's too cold for me." I did not realize that God was sharing with me where I would be... well, you guessed it; I now live in Tennessee and have lived here for years, and I love it! We have a blended family (perhaps another book), and I could not be happier. God has replaced everything that the enemy took, and He continues to bless.

Divorce can appear to be a rough road to travel, but as you navigate it, know that it also presents an opportunity for new beginnings. Understand that your healing and growth will require patience and faith, and there will be many adjustments along the way. However, when you let God do the driving and trust Him, your destination is always ... PERFECT! May you find peace and joy in the journey ahead.

Bobbie Huskey

I pray that you will continue to heal and grow in your faith in Christ. For more information on starting a Divorce Medics Small Group, contact bhuskeyfromhousetohome@gmail.com, or for more information on additional spiritual growth books and CDs, go to: www.davidhuskeyministries.org

Follow on Instagram: traumacoach2024

Follow on TicTok: traumacoach2024

If you enjoy reading this book, please consider leaving a review on the platform from which you purchased it. If you have received a free copy of this book, please consider visiting an online platform to review it. It is a compliment for every author to have reviews, as they allow potential readers to understand what they can expect when reading the book.

Blessings, and thank you for purchasing Divorce Medics.

ANSWER KEY:

PG 14

1. Guard
2. False
3. Is in you
4. Will
5. Weakness
6. Antidote
7. Challenges

PG 28

1. Sleep
2. Any of the following are examples: fear, rest, cognitive dysfunction, loneliness, sadness, and our emotions.
3. Judgmental
4. Support group
5. True

PG 39

1. Denial
2. Defense
3. Real
4. Any of the following are examples: finances, dividing property, tax issues, child support, parental time, healthcare, retirement
5. Your ex

PG 39 cont.

    6. Pros and cons

    7. Support group or counseling

PG 48

1. Examples: Prayer, gym, walking, hiking, yoga, playing an instrument
2. Pray
3. Deception
4. Compassion
5. Serotonin

PG 61

1. Lead to more
2. Peace
3. Insecurities
4. Crushes
5. Let go of it

PG 69

1. Two
2. Normal
3. Examples: changes in beliefs, taking a new job, changes in spending habits, and a decrease in outings with friends
4. True
5. Good
6. Faith

PG 81

1. Thee (you), forsake
2. Wonderfully
3. God
4. Thing
5. Me
6. Peace
7. Decrease

(Personal choice)

PG 90

1. satan
2. Armor
3. Prayer
4. True
5. Prayer

PG 101

1. Spiritual warfare
2. You can change
3. Christ
4. Journal
5. Past
6. Jewel
7. Awesomely or wonderfully

PG 112

1. Actions
2. Antagonistic
3. Peace
4. True
5. Loneliness
6. Active
7. Answers
8. You
9. Righteous man (or woman)

PG 121

1. Understanding
2. Flood
3. Love God
4. By the Lord
5. Ashes

(personal decision)

References:

Firm, G. L. (2024, January 29). How Common Has Divorce Been in Recent Years? Retrieved from Gifford Law Firm : https://www.treasurecoastlawfirm.com/blog/2024/01/howcommon-has-divorce-been-in-recent-years

Hannah Mulholland, L.M. (2024, August 26). Tips for Co-Parenting After Divorce. Retrieved from Mayo Clinic: https://mcpress.mayoclinic.org/parenting/tips-for-co-parenting-after-divorce/

Huskey, D. G. (2019). Start 2 Finish. Sweetwater, TN: David Huskey Ministries.

incorporated, M. W. (2019). Retrieved from Merriam-Webster Dictionary: https://www.merriam-webster.com/dictionary/acceptance

Issa, E. E. (2016, August 25). Nerdwallet. Retrieved from NerdWallet Compare, Inc: https://www.nerdwallet.com/blog/finance/payingbills-time-survey-shows-bad/

Mark Banschick, M. (2013, April 10). The Traumatic Divorce: 6 Ways to Heal. Retrieved from HuffPost: https://www.huffpost.com/entry/the-traumatic-divorce-6w_b_2593381

Means, F. (2024). What Are the Effects of Divorce on Children? Retrieved from familymeans.org: https://familymeans.org/effects-of-divorceon-children.html

mckinleyirvin. (2012, October 30). 32 Shocking Divorce Statistics. Retrieved from www.mckinleyirvin.com: https://www.mckinleyirvin.com/family-law-blog/2012/october/32shocking-divorce-statistics/#_edn3

Miller, L. (2022). Cooperating with Kingdom Principles. Athens, TN: Ascension Life School of Mininstry.

Stanton, G. (2012, September 25). FactChecker: Divorce Rate Among Christians. Retrieved from The Gospel Coalition: https://www.thegospelcoalition.org/article/factchecker-divorcerate-among-christians/

The Holy Bible, Amplified Version. YouVersion App, Version 1.0, YouVersion and One Hope, inc.

The Holy Bible, Amplified Classic Version YouVersion App, Version 1.0, YouVersion and One Hope, inc.

References:

The Holy Bible, Beren Standard Version. YouVersion App, Version 1.0, YouVersion and One Hope, inc.

The Holy Bible, English Standard Version. YouVersion App, Version 1.0, YouVersion and One Hope, inc.

The Holy Bible, King James Version. YouVersion App, Version 1.0, YouVersion and One Hope, inc.

The Holy Bible, New International Version. YouVersion App, Version 1.0, YouVersion and One Hope, inc.

The Holy Bible, New King James Version. YouVersion App, Version 1.0, YouVersion and One Hope, inc.

The Holy Bible, New Living Translation Version. YouVersion App, Version 1.0, YouVersion and One Hope, inc.

www.ingramcontent.com/pod-product-compliance
Lightning Source LLC
Chambersburg PA
CBHW020500030426
42337CB00011B/170